W9-AUM-954

SCIENCE AND THE SEARCH FOR GOD

Gary Kowalski

Lantern Books • New York
A Division of Booklight Inc.

2003
Lantern Books
One Union Square West, Suite 201
New York, NY 10003

© Gary Kowalski 2003

Printed in the United States of America

Library of Congress Cataloging-in-Publication Data

Kowalski, Gary A.
  Science and the search for God / Gary Kowalski.
      p. cm.
Includes bibliographical references.
  ISBN 1-59056-045-0 (alk. paper)
  1. Religion and science. 2. Creation. I. Title.
  BL240.3 .K69 2003
  215--dc21

                                    2002154079

printed on 100% post-consumer waste paper, chlorine-free

"A human being is a part of the whole called by us universe, a part limited in time and space. He experiences himself, his thoughts and feelings as something separated from the rest, a kind of optical delusion of his consciousness. This delusion is a kind of prison for us, restricting us to our personal desires and to affection for a few persons nearest to us. Our task must be to free ourselves from this prison by widening our circle of compassion to embrace all living creatures and the whole of nature in its beauty."

Albert Einstein (1879–1955)

CONTENTS

The cleavage between science and religion has haunted our world for four centuries. Our culture has become soul-sick as a consequence. Nothing could be more important than healing this historic schism, for our technologically driven, spiritually fragmented world can no longer afford either heartless science or mindless faith.

The warfare of science and theology led to an intellectual truce forged by Schleiermacher and his followers: science would deal with objective, external realities, religion with the interior, subjective realm. The religious beliefs that survived this shaky cease-fire seemed weak and often contradictory. But twentieth century advances in physics may be bridging the previously distinct realms of "subjec-

*tive" and "objective" reality, laying the basis for a new
conversation between the two camps.*

Our human fascination with celestial events and heavenly occurrences appears to be universal and may hold a clue to our relationship with the cosmos. The universe is not alien or indifferent to our humanity, but is our native soil and the cradle of our dreams. Hence the religion of the next millennium will find its inspiration, not in the domain of the supernatural, but rather in oneness with the natural world.

Galileo's mechanics represented a major advance in science, but also seemed to divest the world of any significant purpose. But the anthropic principle, as articulated by leading physicists like John Wheeler and Freeman Dyson, indicates the universe may indeed have a purpose in mind. After Galileo, we can no longer believe that people or the planet Earth reside at the center of creation. But science suggests that, in the cosmic scheme, human beings still have an important role to play.

The ideology of materialism is antiquated, owing more to Biblical myth and Greek metaphysics than to current scientific research. Yet the notion that the universe is com-

posed of blind, unthinking matter still holds sway. But could random, brainless forces have fashioned the elegant equations that describe reality at its fundamental levels? Both science and faith demand a better answer to the question, "What is the world made of?"

Geologists, oceanographers, climatologists and others who look at the big picture are beginning to realize that life is a property, not of molecules, genes or even individual organisms, but of whole planetary systems. Will the Gaia Hypothesis lead to renewed reverence and respect for our fragile Mother Earth? If so, the change couldn't happen too soon.

Darwin hesitated to publish his theory of evolution for fear it would undermine religious belief. But even confirmed skeptics like paleontologist Stephen Jay Gould are subject to feelings of awe and astonishment in the presence of the intricate dance of life. Such mystical or "peak" experiences are entirely appropriate, leading us to honor and celebrate the evolutionary dance that carries us in its unfolding.

Science claims to examine the world dispassionately. But the work of three leading primatologists — all women — suggests that emotion and passion have an important place in any scientific investigation. The heart has wisdom that an excessively "heady" approach to the natural sciences desperately needs if we are to save the world's endangered species — including our own.

The framework of process philosophy, first developed by Alfred North Whitehead and elaborated by Charles Hartshorne, provides a way of thinking about the universe that has been outlined in the preceding chapters: a universe where consciousness is finely woven into the fabric of things, where the whole exceeds the parts, and where living relationships connect every corner of the cosmos. The vision of God that arises from this gestalt is ecological, non-patriarchal, and immanent in the world around us.

Mystery is the element in which both science and religion live and move and have their being, and the question of why anything exists at all forever confounds the human intellect. Humility — the opposite of intellectual arrogance — may be one value on which science and faith can converge, for the world will always be infinitely wider than our understanding of it.

Sigmund Freud predicted that religious belief would wither with the advance of science. But God's obituary proved premature, and as science shed the reductionistic, mechanistic constructs that were so inimical to faith, a new synthesis seemed possible. The dialogue between scientists and theologians is now gearing up. Our journey of faith is just beginning.

ABOUT THIS BOOK

This book is intended for open-minded people of all beliefs who wonder how to square the findings of science with the teachings of their own spiritual traditions.

For the intellectually curious, it offers a brief, non-technical introduction to a few of the cutting-edge ideas in cosmology and the life sciences. For those interested in whether God can be found anywhere amid the latest bulletins about genomes and black holes, it provides a quick entry point to process theology — one of the more promising developments in recent religious discourse that aims to bridge the gap between the universe of science and the universe of faith.

The reader will encounter no equations or complicated diagrams within these pages. The facts are current and the scientific theories contained here are accurately represented, but the language used is evocative and at times even inspirational. One critic complained about this, arguing that poetic descriptions of the world are less than fully objective. But the assumption that lifeless, impersonal prose is the most precise way of talking about things implies that reality at its core is also impersonal and drab. And it is exactly this presumption — that the cosmos is lacking in personality, inhospitable to lyricism and flights of fancy — that this book is designed to combat.

"Junk science" has no place in this discussion. Some of the concepts presented here, like the Big Bang, are so well established that no serious rivals are on the horizon, even though models for a "steady-state" cosmos are still occasionally advanced by reputable astronomers. Other hypotheses, like the anthropic principle, are less widely accepted. But while some of the ideas considered here may be outside the mainstream, none are beyond the fringe. I have no interest in pseudo-science. Religious folk need to wrestle with the challenges posed by science in its toughest, most rigorous format. We may find that like Jacob, who grappled with an angel, we receive an unexpected blessing for our efforts.

Science and the Search for God is not a historical survey or an academic tome. Rather, this work represents the outgrowth of an encounter with my own angels and demons, contending with all the tensions of skepticism and the quest for meaning. As an ordained minister, delving into life's "ultimate questions" is my professional stock-in-trade. But trying to figure out where non-material realities might fit into a purely material world has also been a personal preoccupation of mine for the past quarter-century. As a child, I was filled with certainty. Growing up, I was convinced science had all the answers. When I hit adulthood (or when it hit me, in the form of grief, loss and the other predictable tragedies of living), I realized I needed more light to steer by. And having struggled through a few dark times, glimmerings have dawned. But the conclusions I've reached do not represent the official doctrines of any particular sect. I continue to be inspired by thinkers who are Catholic and Protestant, Buddhist and Jewish, from confirmed secularists like the late Stephen Jay Gould to religious humanists like Albert Einstein.

True believers and die-hard infidels will both find ample room to quarrel with this approach. But my aim is not to provoke controversy so much as to encourage honest conversation. Surely people of good will can be allowed differing notions of the divine. And for this reason, I have included a list of "issues for discussion" at the end of this volume. This particular book had its origin in a class on "Topics in Science and Religion" that I developed for my own congregation. And my hope is that readers might want to form study circles within their own churches and synagogues, using this work as the basis for dialogue and reflection. If *Science and the Search for God* raises as many questions as it answers, my goal will have been achieved.

I want to thank the members of my parish, the First Unitarian Universalist Society of Burlington, for encouraging me to be as clear and open as possible in the articulation of my own doubts and affirmations. Special gratitude goes to those with scientific expertise who were kind enough to read and comment on my manuscript. These include Beal Hyde, professor emeritus in genetics at the University of Vermont, Professor Henry Steffens, specializing in the history of science at UVM, Don Manley, professor of astronomy at UVM, and his wife, Peteranne Joel, who teaches biochemistry at the same institution. Cyrus Bryant, professor of physics at Johnson State College, was an indispensable consultant, while Phil Goodman and my daughter Holly Jones offered valuable help with research. I am additionally indebted to the dozens of people who listened to me lecture at the Naramata Summer Institute and contributed their suggestions. I want to express my appreciation to Martin Rowe, my editor at Lantern Books, for his support, and I cannot forget my wife, Dori Jones, whose patience endured through numerous drafts. Some gave more barbs than kudos, but to them I am especially grateful, for surely this is what both scientists and theologians need for the integrity of their work—faithful critics.

Reverend Gary Kowalski

HEALING THE BLIND, CURING THE LAME

"Which is More Dangerous: Science or Religion?" I did a double take when a friend handed me a newspaper clipping with that headline. It was an ad from an organization called The Great American Think-Off, which posed the question as the subject for its annual Philosophy Competition. Reading more, I learned that contestants were invited to submit opinions in the form of an essay of 750 words or less, with a monetary award and book contract promised to those with the best answers.

Maybe my friend thought I might want to enter the contest. But while the idea of a philosophy competition has a quaint appeal, this one to me seemed deliberately misleading. Isn't it possible that science and religion are allies rather than antagonists? Doesn't the real peril arise when the two are seen as stark alternatives rather than as natural partners? The timing of the contest, on the edge of the twenty-first century, was an alarming indication that the warfare between science and religion—a running skirmish for the past four hundred years—is still unresolved and spilling over now into a whole new millennium.

Some trace the beginning of the battle back to 1600, when the Italian philosopher Giordano Bruno was burned at the stake for teaching that the universe is infinite. Ahead of his time, Bruno postulated that each of the shimmering points of light in the night sky might be a sun just like our own. Perhaps every one had its own ring of planets, inhabited by intelligent beings. For that heresy, he had an iron rod driven through his tongue prior to his immolation.

But you needn't go digging far into the annals of the past to see science and religion in conflict. To savor the paradox, tune in to any modern televangelist, preaching a literal interpretation of the Bible, broadcasting his message on electromagnetic waves that would have been as baffling to the authors of the scriptures as the Book of Revelation seems to us today. As we enter the era of the global village, science provides the unifying story for a world that has become linked through technology. The internet, cell phones and TV may be the most noisy, visible tokens of the emerging planetary culture, but the gadgetry rests on an underlying knowledge of the properties of electrons and other laws of nature. The Bible-believing Christian or ultra-orthodox Jew, putting on his glasses to read from the book of Genesis, is relying on the same rules of optics that astronomers use to tell us that the universe could not possibly have been created the way the Good Book says.

The languages of mathematics and the physical sciences are the *lingua franca* that offer a universal medium of communication among the world's varied peoples. But even as the population of the planet grows closer together via the wonders of transistors, the world remains divided in its religious traditions. There are almost two billion Christians living on Earth at present, over a billion Muslims, 840 million Hindus and 320 million Buddhists, each of them inheritors of a spiritual legacy that is thousands of years old and utterly pre-scientific in outlook.

Since the epoch when our early human ancestors first bowed before the mystery of existence, devising the most primitive rituals of placation against the unknown, religion has been with us. For four thousand years, observes Karen Armstrong, the idea of God has "constantly adapted to meet the demands of the present, but in our own century, more and more people have found that it no longer works for them, and when religious ideas cease to be effective they fade away. Maybe God really is an idea of the past." Ninety-five percent of the biologists in the prestigious National Academy of Sciences call themselves atheists or agnostics, suggesting Armstrong might be right. Yet an even greater percentage of laypeople affirm some belief in a Supreme Being, while a third of all Americans profess that they have been "born again." If theism is waning among the scientifically educated, belief in God remains more fervent than ever among the religious rank and file. Yet religion in its archaic dress can no longer offer a compelling explanation of how our cosmos operates or came to be.

There are also limits to the explanatory power of science, however. Those limits became plain to me a few years back when the Hubble Space Telescope malfunctioned on launch, requiring emergency repairs from the crew aboard the Space Shuttle. The moment of insight came when I heard the astronauts were relying on alligator clips, wire, and duct tape to try to repair the situation. It occurred to me that there are basically two kinds of problems we face as human beings: those that can be solved with duct tape and those that can't. And while I would never dream of disparaging the utility of the sticky gray roll that hangs in my broom closet, neither would I expect it to help me be a better parent, give comfort to the

bereaved or offer peace of mind in times of inward per-
plexity. Tape can't repair a broken heart, and no wire clip-
pers are sharp enough to cut through a moral dilemma.
Such challenges can never be met through science; they
require the cultivation of love, serenity, discernment and
wisdom, which are all the province of religion.

But what kind of religion is adequate to provide
guidance for our times? Can the metaphysics of the
Greeks or Hebrews help us navigate the universe of
quarks and neutrinos, of relativity and quantum theory?
The struggle to find an accommodation between ancient
myth and modern insight has not been easy, driving
many individuals into the arms of bad science and bogus
religion. Fundamentalism, narrow-minded and intolerant, is proliferating among almost all of the world's great
faiths. Meanwhile, the number of people who give cre-
dence to astrology, numerology and other *ersatz* "sciences" is growing. The success of cults like Heaven's
Gate, whose followers committed mass suicide in the
belief that they would be transported to a flying saucer
hidden behind a passing comet, indicates how willing
some people are to let themselves be deluded, at least if
the delusion has a coating of space-age spirituality.

Delusions of any kind are dangerous, but those that
stem from the cleavage of faith and reason are especially
so, for if religion has the power to unleash the best and

worst in human nature, science has the ability to harness the creative and destructive potential of nature itself. Poised so precariously upon the brink, the world can no longer afford either heartless science or mindless faith. Religion, in its root meaning, comes from the Latin verb *religare*, which means "to bind together." The function of religion is to provide unity and coherence to our experience of the world, but for too long that experience has been compartmentalized and divided between fact and feeling, the natural and supernatural, the truths discovered in the laboratory and those proclaimed in the temple. How much of the insanity around us stems from this schizophrenic split?

One wonders. Would those in our acquisitive consumer culture be so driven to endlessly multiply possessions if they could find more meaningful spiritual satisfactions in their daily lives? Would so many require therapy, or would depression be so widespread, if people had access to a healthier, more sustaining worldview to give purpose to their existence? Would alcoholism and addiction be so endemic if more people could experience the highs — the joy, acceptance and inward peace — that a workable faith can provide? Would our environment be in such peril if science could not only explain the world, but teach us to love and care for it as well?

Ours has been called the "information age," for the wealth of technical knowledge at our command has never been greater. Specialized journals abound for ecology, ethology, endocrinology and even exobiology. But there are few connecting or unifying themes that could give these separate sub-plots some sense of being part of the same story. And it's still less evident how the latest scientific bulletins about pulsars or elementary particles relate to our own life stories or matters of daily interest. We have as a result a series of "factoids" and headlines without context or much sense of what is genuinely important, a culture that is rich in know-how, but that has almost forgotten the answers to the most vital questions of all, of who we are, where we come from and how we relate to the larger scheme of things. Religion has traditionally provided the storyline that, in the words of philosopher Hannah Arendt, "reveals the meaning of what otherwise would remain an unbearable sequence of sheer happenings." Lacking any sacred narrative to provide the answers, people now turn to profane sources to tell them who they are: advertising, movies and the media. The popularity of entertainment like *Star Wars* probably springs from the film's not-too-subtle mythic overtones. But Hollywood isn't likely to supply any lasting sense of purpose for the masses who now feel directionless and confused. For that, a more authentic story is required.

Every preacher knows that one good story is better than a heap of dry data. To give a personal example, I remember how my own brother struggled to learn the periodic chart when he was studying chemistry in high school. There are over a hundred elements, each with its own symbol, and while some are easy to remember (who could forget that H stands for hydrogen?), others are not intuitively obvious. My brother was having particular trouble with mercury, whose sign is Hg, until my mother told him a story. "Where do we find mercury?" she asked and answered her own query, "In thermometers. What does the mercury in a thermometer do?"

"It goes up. What else goes up? Helium balloons go up. What is the most famous story about a helium balloon ever written? *Around the World in Eighty Days*. And who wrote that tale? H.G. Wells," she concluded triumphantly—"and that is how to remember that the symbol for mercury is Hg!" I have never forgotten the symbol for mercury, and I doubt my brother has, either, even though Jules Verne was the actual author of *Around the World in Eighty Days*. Even a made-up story is better than none.

What we desperately need at this point in history, however, are true stories—stories that can rejoin *mythos* with *logos,* reminding us not only of the names of the elements, but of why any of it matters. The old epics — the Bible, the Koran, the Upanishads — were grand and still have much to teach us. But none is up to the challenges that face our planet in the next thousand years. From genetic engineering to space exploration, the risks and opportunities ahead are unprecedented. Outmoded legends will not do. For the new millennium, fresh stories are needed — non-fiction narratives that are based in realism, but that also offer hope and sustenance for the human spirit.

Such a story is now beginning to emerge, born of the latest discoveries in biology and physics. This new story offers humankind less reason than ever to feel special, unique or privileged within the natural order. No longer can *Homo sapiens* regard itself as the finale or capstone of creation. At the same time, this new narrative provides solid ground for feeling at one and at home with the rest of nature. If the human species has lost the exalted position heralded in the Psalms — "a little lower than the angels" — neither are we condemned to wander through time as accidental tourists or mere creatures of cosmic happenstance. For when we lift our eyes toward the Big Picture, we glimpse a reflection of our own humanity — a universe where consciousness, caring and creativity, the things that give life meaning, are built into the very foundations of existence.

These pages are intended as a précis of this new narrative, my own response to the challenge of the "think-off" proffered by my friend. Consider this book less a roadmap toward the reconciliation of science and religion—for parts of that route are still under construction—than as a series of scenic turnouts along the way. Each chapter offers a separate vista. But by the end of the volume, the reader may have some sense of how these various vantage points converge to reveal a single panorama. Without laboriously covering every inch of the territory, we will see how science and faith really do share a common terrain—as distinct promontories, to be sure, but both rooted in the same upthrusting range of truth.

Which is more dangerous: science or religion—or the notion that the two can somehow function in splendid isolation from each other? We must discover a means to reunite these two ways of knowing, the ancient and the modern. For as Einstein once said, religion without science is blind; science without religion is lame.

TELL ME WHY

2

There is a song you may have sung once upon a time, in Sunday School, at summer camp or around the piano at home. It's a simple tune, childlike and reassuring in its belief that life has a purpose and that the world is in good hands. The words and music are familiar:

Tell me why the stars do shine.
Tell me why the ivy twines.
Tell me why the sky is blue.
Then I will tell you just why I love you.

The second verse, of course, provides the answers, answers that once seemed plausible and comforting and may still waken a small stirring in the heart, even if our minds can no longer accept such easy explanations for why the universe is the way it is:

11

Because God made the stars to shine,
Because God made the ivy twine,
Because God made the sky so blue,
Because God made you, that's why I love you.

Now that we know that nuclear fusion, the melding of hydrogen atoms into helium, is what burns inside the heart of stars, the cosmos seems less intimate, not as friendly as it once did. We have harnessed that stellar energy now, for good or ill. We've penetrated the thin envelope of blue that encircles our small planet and looked into the black depths of space, inhospitable, cold and seemingly hostile to the twining ivy and most other forms of life. Gone is the innocent sense of being at home in a world that was made expressly for our enjoyment.

Yet in the not too distant past, it was still possible for educated and intelligent people to believe that the heavens declared the glory of God, that a loving providence had hung the sun in the sky to give light by day and the stars like lanterns in the night. Science was the ally of religion. When Sir Isaac Newton died in 1727, for example, he was convinced that his greatest achievements were not in the realm of physics but rather of theology, for indeed the two realms seemed inseparable. To read more deeply into the book of nature was to understand the thoughts of its divine author. At the conclusion of his *Principia*, Newton reflected that "this most beautiful system of the sun, planets and comets could only proceed from the counsel and dominion of an intelligent and powerful Being." The laws of motion, after all, appeared to demand a lawgiver. The great world machine required a chief engineer to design it and set it running. Indeed, Sir Isaac's apologetic concerns sometimes got the better of his scientific program. "When I wrote my treatise about our system," he confided in a letter to Richard Bentley, "I had an eye upon such principles as might work with considering men for the belief in Deity." And it was a particular kind of Deity that Newton favored, God as Master Mechanic, who took inert materials, fashioned them into a semblance of order and set the flywheels turning. This was not a divinity intimately involved in the messiness of human relations or the earthiness of living. God was as distant and far removed from creation as an eighteenth-century monarch from the daily lives of the subjects who ploughed his fields. But the sovereign's existence could be deduced from the world's smooth governance—the argument from design. In the words of Joseph Addison's famous hymn of that era,

The spacious firmament on high,
With all the blue ethereal sky,
And spangled heavens, a shining frame,
Their great Original proclaim.

Yet in the clockwork universe that was taking shape, God was becoming increasingly extraneous. When the mathematician Laplace presented Napoleon with a copy of his work on *Celestial Mechanics*, the emperor said to him, "You have written this huge work on the heavens without once mentioning God," to which Laplace calmly replied, "Sire, I had no need of that hypothesis." Slowly, like a Cheshire cat, the face of the Creator was receding from the cosmos, leaving only a mocking grin.

But if God as a hypothesis was increasingly unnecessary, religion as a source of succor and psychological support was still very much needed and could not merely fade away. Rather, its locus changed, from outer space to inner, and as the universe round about came to seem less personal, religion became more so. The German theologian Friedrich Schleiermacher (1768–1834) did most to internalize matters of faith when he defined religion as "the feeling of absolute dependence." By narrowing religion to a feeling, Schleiermacher sequestered and saved it from the assaults of scientific inquiry. Faith was understood less as a set of propositions about objective reality than as an inward condition of confidence and trust. Henceforth theologians would surrender their claim to speak about the public world of observable phenomena and speak instead to the private realm of sentiment and emotion: hope and despair, joy and anguish. There would be a division of labor, scientists dealing with things that could be weighed and measured, clergy dealing with the intangible domain of meaning and value.

Most of the forward-looking faithful followed Schleiermacher's lead. Major theologians in twentieth-century Protestant circles included figures like Paul Tillich and Rudolf Bultmann, who sought to "de-mythologize" the message of the scriptures. For Bultmann, this meant the Bible was not primarily a sourcebook of history or physics, but a document intended to bring men and women to a point of personal decision about how to live. Tillich preferred the term "de-literalize," but likewise argued that religion "must leave to science the description of the whole of objects and their interdependence in nature and history." In "Science and Theology: A Discussion with Einstein," Tillich said the idea of a Personal God, intervening in the world or meddling with its laws, was passé. Such obsolescent images would make the deity "a natural object beside others, an object among objects, a being among beings, maybe the highest, but nevertheless *a* being." Tillich encouraged his readers to consider God as the ground of Being itself—a depth and abyss that could be sensed, not in events of the natural world, but rather in "the experience of the numinous," i.e. in the realm of religious feeling. Other theologians like Karl Barth returned to revelation as the final arbiter of religious authority and simply ignored science as a pursuit that had nothing to do with the propositions of faith, whose truth claims stood outside of time and beyond the sphere of sensory confirmation. "Natural theology," which sought to adduce empirical support for religious belief, fell into disfavor, for there seemed to be so little in the natural world to validate traditional ideas of God. And so theology, which once styled itself "the queen of the sciences," became increasingly ingrown. By the middle of the twentieth century, the two camps had ceased even to be rivals or sparring partners. Rather, scientists and theologians had simply stopped speaking to each other.

Ironically, it was the religious reactionaries who refused to accept the division of labor, continuing to insist that faith rest upon the basis of testable evidence. So today it is the fundamentalist who is most interested in carbon dating the Shroud of Turin, for example, or in gathering fossil data to support the hypothesis of a deluge, or "scientific creationism." The modernist looks on these ventures as misguided or irrelevant, since his or her religious convictions in no way depend on the historicity of Noah or the flood. Even the recent discovery of an ossuary or burial casket from the early first century inscribed with the name of "James, son of Joseph, brother of Jesus" roused little stir among mainline

Christians, for archaeology—as a science—presumably has little to say to the tenets of faith. By the same token, few progressively minded theologians were perturbed when the famous Shroud, supposedly the burial garment of Jesus, turned out to be a fourteenth-century forgery. Whatever they thought about Easter, few supposed it was the kind of event that left behind a trail of radioactive isotopes that could be documented in the lab.

But there is a price to be paid for the truce the liberal makes with science. The cost is relativism, or at least a lack of firm resolution in some core convictions. For if religion and science are truly separate enterprises, dealing with entirely different dimensions of experience, where do religious intuitions touch down in the hard world of fact? Nobel Prize-winning physicist Stephen Weinberg put the matter strongly, but he does have a point when he writes that "many religious liberals today seem to think that different people can believe in different mutually exclusive things without any of them being wrong, as long as their beliefs 'work for them.' This one believes in reincarnation, that one in heaven and hell; a third believes in the extinction of the soul at death, but no one can be said to be wrong as long as everyone gets a satisfying spiritual rush." While tolerance is commendable, how seriously can we take a religious stance that tolerates nonsense or absurdities within its own ranks?

Says Weinberg, "Religious liberals are in one sense even farther in spirit from scientists than are fundamentalists and other religious conservatives. At least the conservatives, like the scientists, tell you that they believe in what they believe because it is true, rather than because it makes them good or happy."

Few people, though, whether conservative or liberal, would agree that we can be virtuous or happy and completely self-deceiving at the same time. No rational person knowingly accepts falsehood as the truth, and few are willing to abandon their wits unless it's altogether necessary. Yet it remains a challenge to know what we honestly can believe when scientists like Weinberg tell us that "the more we learn about our universe, the more it all seems pointless."

Fortunately, that dreary conclusion is not shared by all. Many of our greatest modern scientists are rather inclined to concur with the astronomer James Jeans (1877–1946), when he wrote:

> *Fifty years ago, the universe was generally looked on as a machine; it was said that the final aim of science was to explain all the objects in the world, including living bodies, as machines, as mere jumbles of atoms which would perform mechanical dances for a time under the action of blind, purposeless forces and then*

fall back to form a dead world. Modern science gives but little support to such materialistic views. When we pass to extremes of size in either direction — whether to the cosmos as a whole, or to the inner recesses of the atom — the mechanical interpretation of Nature fails. We come to entities and phenomena which are in no sense mechanical. To me they seem less suggestive of mechanical than of mental processes; the universe seems to be nearer to a great thought than to a great machine.

The image of the universe as a great thought is more than mere metaphor. As Jeans suggests, both of the major revolutions in twentieth-century physics acknowledged consciousness, whose presence had previously been relegated to the purely subjective, as a potent force within the universe. The Special Theory of Relativity asserted that such seemingly objective realities as mass and velocity, distance and duration, can shrink and expand depending on the reference point of the observer. The measurement of time and space varies according to who is doing the measuring. Quantum theory, the other paradigm shift of modern science, holds that on the atomic level, as well, perception plays an important part in determining what is perceived. If it's true that mind is not merely an accident or aberration in the cosmos, but stitched into the very fabric of being, it means that we human beings, although very small and seemingly insignificant within the vast scope of creation, are not at all strangers or exiles within the universe, but deeply at home here, integrally connected to all that is. And if Jeans' description is accurate, then the demarcation between the world and our apprehension of the world—the outward expanse of science and the inward sanctum assigned to faith—is less hard-and-fast than once supposed. The line between fact and feeling begins to soften.

Inner space—our subjective sense of selfhood and personal interiority—is just as durable and firm as the outward world of rocks and rivers and other items that can been seen and touched. That would seem to be what Erwin Schrödinger (1887–1961), one of the founders of quantum mechanics, was trying to say in his book *What Is Life?*, a volume that helped inspire the revolution in genetics that followed World War II. Schrödinger was one of a small group of physicists (others included Max Delbrück of Cal Tech and Seymour Benzer at the University of California in La Jolla) who felt that inquiries at the quantum level had reached an impasse and in the late 1940s turned their attention to biology, to learn whether any fundamentally new properties of nature might be discovered in living beings. Mostly, they found that organic systems could be explained without resort to any *elan vitale* or insubstantial essence. Yet consciousness itself seemed to be an exception to the rule—a datum of experience that could not be reduced to any simpler physical components.

In a meditation on necessity and free will, Schrödinger set forth the two apparently contradictory propositions that 1) *My body functions as a pure mechanism according to the Laws of Nature,* and 2) *Yet I know, by incontrovertible personal experience, that I am directing its motions.* The statements, he observed, appear irrefutable but mutually exclusive. The only logically consistent way to reconcile them is with the wild surmise that I—"I" in the widest possible aspect—am the one directing the Laws of Nature. Schrödinger elaborated with the following blend of thought experiment and guided fantasy:

> *Suppose you are sitting on a bench beside a path in high mountain country. There are grassy slopes all around, with rocks jutting through them; on the opposite slope of the valley there is a stretch of scree with a low growth of alder bushes. Woods climb steeply on both sides of the valley, up to the line of treeless pasture; and facing you, soaring up from the depths of the valley, is the mighty, glacier-tipped peak, its smooth snow-fields and hard-edged rock-faces touched at this moment with soft rose-color by the last rays of the*

departing sun, all marvelously sharp against the clear,
pale, transparent sky.

Sitting here, you realize that the landscape is ancient. For thousands of years, the rocks, the woods and glaciers have existed and so, with minor changes, they will continue to exist for ages after your own footprints have long since faded from human memory. For generations, men and women have suffered and struggled for survival, given birth and vanished into the obscurity of time. A hundred years ago, perhaps another person sat in the very spot that you now occupy, like you wistful in the lingering light, his or her heart equally filled with joy at the beauty of the day, equally anxious at the inevitable descent of night. Who was this other person, Schrödinger asks. *"Was it someone else? Was it not you yourself? What is this Self of yours?"* The questions seem to answer themselves, Schrödinger declares: the consciousness in you is the selfsame awareness that exists in other beings and that has existed throughout all time. The ego's sensation of separateness masks a more profound identity. "Thus you can throw yourself flat on the ground, stretched out upon Mother Earth, with the certain conviction that you are one with her and she with you," Schrödinger exclaimed.

*You are as firmly established, as invulnerable as she,
indeed a thousand times firmer and more invulnerable.
As surely as she will engulf you tomorrow, so surely
will she bring you forth anew to a new striving and
suffering. And not merely 'some day': now, today,
every day she is bringing you forth, not once but thousands upon thousands of times, just as every day she
engulfs you a thousand times over. For eternally and
always there is only now, one and the same now; the
present is the only thing that has no end.*

From the detail of the description, it is hard to believe
that Schrödinger was not being autobiographical. High
in the mountain pass, in the dying light, he had experi-
enced what Schleiermacher called "creature-feeling."
How brief his own lifespan seemed amid the slow-mov-
ing tide of glacial seas, how meager his puny frame
beneath the crush of towering peaks and endless sky!
But like thousands of others who have had similar peak
experiences, he also had a flashing insight into a secret
that the sober mood of science misses. At such moments,
religion is not so much a feeling that we have as a feeling
that has us: a vivid awareness of kinship and affinity
with a life larger and more lasting than our own.

Steven Weinberg is right up to a point; we are not
permitted to believe things merely because they make us

feel good. Religion, in my opinion, should never presume to contradict the findings of physics or chemistry or geology. At the same time, faith has every right to go beyond science, forming conjectures that can never be proven or falsified, which may even appear to contradict themselves. Thus a part of me agrees with Einstein, when he wrote that "I cannot imagine a God who rewards and punishes the objects of his creation ... Neither can I believe that the individual survives the death of his body." Yet another part of me kindles to the thoughts the great physicist expressed in 1955, when he learned that his closest friend, Michele Besso, had died. In a letter of condolence to Besso's sister and son, Einstein wrote, "Now he has departed this strange world a little ahead of me. That means nothing. People like us, who believe in physics, know that the distinction between past, present and future is only a stubbornly persistent illusion."

The quotation at the front of this book comes from another letter of Einstein's, this one to a nineteen-year-old girl who had lost a much-loved younger sister and wanted to know what solace a scientist might be able to offer, since she could find no comfort in traditional religious concepts. Einstein's affirmation that the ego is only an "optical delusion of consciousness" is reminiscent of Schrödinger's ruminations, and like Schrödinger,

Einstein suggested that release from pain and spiritual freedom might be attained through a deeper realization of life's genuine and abiding unity. "No one is able to achieve this completely," he wrote, "but the striving for such achievement is in itself a part of the liberation and a foundation for inner security."

Who am I to say that Einstein was wrong to offer sympathy or reach for comfort when faced with such a loss? Who can say what happens when we die, and who can live without hope? Perhaps the most important thing that science can teach us is how much we do not know, schooling us in humility, while at the same time reminding us of the vast unknown in which we exist. As long as the stars shine, we will continue to ask why we are here and how it all began. As long as the ivy twines, we will wonder how life can be so beautiful, or so brief. The certainties of childhood may be gone, but the questions will remain as long as the sky is blue. And without knowing the final answers, we can still hear the music.

STAR DUST

3

James Luther Adams relates the story of the minister of a small congregation in an old New England mill town who once every year treated the worshipers at his church to a long-winded sermon on astronomy, detailing everything that had been discovered about the stars and planets during the preceding twelve months. His parishioners — cotton brokers, bankers, weavers and other down-to-earth sorts — sat through this annual ordeal with patient resignation. Finally someone asked him, "What is the use of knowing so much about the far reaches of empty space?" To which the minister replied, "No use at all, but it greatly enlarges my idea of God."

Were I in the custom of delivering sermons of the kind described, my own flock would have been in for a lengthy listening experience at the end of 1997, a year of celestial blockbusters. That spring, there was the spectacle of Comet Hale-Bopp, revisiting the night skies after its previous appearance four thousand years before. In the summer, headlines were filled with news of the ill-fated space station Mir, recording the drama of the Russian and American crew members who struggled to keep the damaged ship aloft. And when the Mars Pathfinder bounced down onto the floodplain of an ancient Martian river in July, over one hundred million people summoned up images of the event on the Jet Propulsion Laboratory's website, to watch a little robot nicknamed "Sojourner" roll across the dusty landscape and take samples of the rust colored rocks. Movie theaters packed them in with flicks like *Contact*, based on Carl Sagan's fictional account of the first human encounter with life forms beyond the solar system, but as usual the film wasn't as good as the novel, and in this case the novel wasn't as good as the real thing. America's attention seemed to be shifting heavenward once more, suddenly worried that asteroids like the one that killed the dinosaurs might be whirling this way, but also tantalized and curious about the possibilities of space exploration, fascinated by the question of what (or who) might be out there.

The biggest story that emerged is that we may not be alone. When my son Noah, in fourth grade at that time, showed me his homework one afternoon, one of the questions asked, "How many planets are there?" I knew that "nine" was the answer the teacher wanted. That was the number I had learned in school. But I dimly realized the answer was no longer entirely correct. Not long ago, Michel Mayor and Didier Queloz, two astronomers at an observatory in Geneva, Switzerland, discovered another planet, roughly the size of Jupiter, orbiting a star in the constellation of Pegasus, approximately forty light years from Earth. That discovery clinched what had long been the supposition of most scientists — that planetary systems like the one we inhabit must be widespread in the universe, and that among the millions of planets that presumably exist, many must be suitable homes for life.

Mars, of course, is the best candidate within easy reach, and speculation about what we might find there has ebbed and flowed more often than the red planet's famous polar caps. At the turn of the twentieth century, a group of French scientists offered a prize of 100,000 francs to the first person to communicate with spacemen — with the hitch that contacting Martians wouldn't count, since everyone knew the planet was inhabited anyway. When an American spacecraft snapped the first grainy photographs of the Martian surface back in 1965, the idea that life could thrive on that bleak and barren desert was almost dashed. Hopes were kindled a few years later when Mariner 9 found dry lakebeds and the contours of what had been rivers on Mars. Pessimism set in when a Viking Lander scooped up samples of the dry soil and initially reported signs of biological activity, but the results turned out to be reactions between the soil and substances inside the experimental chambers. The startling report that NASA researchers had discovered microfossils within a chunk of meteorite blown off a Martian mountaintop by some unknown collision 3.6 billion years ago was apparently premature. Some specialists are still unconvinced that these tiny traces, less than one percent the size of any known terrestrial fossils, really represent the remains of living organisms. But the definitive evidence is probably not far off.

Life depends on liquidity. In May of 2002, the Mars Odyssey probe found evidence of frozen water in deposits up to two feet thick around the southern Martian pole, amounting to trillions of gallons in all—more than double the volume of water in Lake Michigan. Presumably that water flowed at one time, and on earth even very cold environments can harbor biological activity. The McMurdo Dry Valleys of Antarctica, at first sight an arid wasteland looking very much like a rubbled Martian plain, contain at least twenty species of photosynthetic bacteria, a like number of algae and a number of invertebrate animals such as mites, springtails and

other diminutive critters at the top of the food chain. All
these "extremophiles" (creatures adapted to adverse
conditions) depend on a brief summer flow of runoff
from surrounding icefields for their sustenance. As for
Mars? "Where there's water, there's life," the director of
the Odyssey project confidently predicts. The jury is still
out, but more missions are scheduled for the near future.
The answer seems to be within close reach.

Harder to answer is the question, "Who cares?" Why
does it matter? Like the parishioner in that New England
congregation who asked his minister why he should be
concerned with so much empty space, we might well ask
what difference it makes whether some single-celled
algae of the type we try so hard to eliminate from our
swimming pools once swam in a vanished Martian sea.
For most of us, the highway construction and traffic jams
we encounter on the way to work affect our lives much
more concretely than any conceivable information that
the Global Surveyor, which recently mapped the terrain
of Mars, yielded about that planet's topography. Still,
some small corner of our being wants to know—and not
only about the mysterious "face" on Mars, a set of features looking weirdly like eyes, nose and a crooked grin,
which the Surveyor's cameras examined in considerable
detail. Some had speculated the face was the remnant of
an ancient civilization. A closer look suggests the features

are nothing more than the products of erosion, like the faces and silhouettes carved out of rock in some of our own national parks. Still, it's pretty cool. Most of us would like to know more about the crags and craters and other natural features that future cameras will reveal. These things may not affect us practically, but they do touch us emotionally and spiritually at some level. But the puzzle remains, "Why?"

One possible answer was given by Piero Coda, a professor of theology at the Vatican in Rome, who recently observed that if life were found on another planet, then those life forms would also have been contaminated by Original Sin and would require salvation (leading me to wonder once more whether there is intelligent life on Earth). A better answer, perhaps, is that such investigations enlarge our idea of God, or, to say much the same thing with less religious baggage, they satisfy our incurable human itch to construct a cosmos of the world we live in, a single, coherent structure of meaning that relates the smallest pebble at our feet to the largest and most distant cluster of stars, that can connect our brief and flickering existence, here on a rocky globe revolving around a mid-sized sun on the outer arms of the Milky Way, to some grander scheme of which we are only a part.

Amid the daily concerns and petty worries that fill our horizon, we occasionally need to lift our eyes to glimpse the Big Picture. In the congregation I currently serve, I've made a habit each Sunday morning of including some brief mention of what stars and planets are visible in the night sky, a weekly almanac of the heavens, and most people tell me it's one of their favorite parts of the service. They like the reminder to watch for the Perseids in August, as well as knowing what constellations are rising in each new season—the great Summer Triangle, for instance—or how to find the nebula in the dagger that hangs from Orion's belt in winter, a glowing, gaseous remnant of a supernova where new stars are even now congealing out of the old. Such information lifts us out of our mundane preoccupations, if only for moment, and reminds us that it's a pretty amazing universe we inhabit. Isn't there a touch of the stargazer in all of us?

Almost every culture boasts ancient observatories, from Stonehenge in England to the Ch'omsongdae in Korea. Many archeologists are convinced that the pyramids of Egypt were modeled on solar imagery, each triangular edifice representing a golden ray of sun. The Mayans, too, built celestial referents into their smaller, stepped pyramids, like the temple of the Feathered Serpent in Chichen Itza, where twin snakes flanking the central staircase cast a series of undulating, serpentine shadows at the instant the sun sets on the day of vernal and autumnal equinox. Such feats of engineering bespeak both a sophisticated understanding of motions of the stars and planets and a general fascination with the upper regions of things. The attraction appears to be as old as civilization itself.

For millennia, people have been looking up at the sky, partly to understand the seasons and cycles of planting and harvest, but mostly for reasons that are less practical than spiritual—because we feel the enchantment of countless points of light scattered across the darkness. Mark Twain had the mood about right:

> *We had the sky up there, all speckled with stars, and we used to discuss about whether they was made or only just happened. Jim allowed they was made, but I allowed they happened; I judged it would have took too long to make so many. Jim said the moon could 'a' laid them; well, that looked kind of reasonable, so I didn't say nothing against it, because I've seen a frog lay most as many, so of course it could be done. We used to watch the stars that fell, too, and see them streak down. Jim allowed they'd got spoiled and was hove out of the nest.*

We may know more about meteors and stellar evolution these days, but looking up at the Seven Sisters, and

Cygnus the Swan, and the Great Bear and her children we still sense forces that are old and vast beyond finding out. It is a strange and mystifying universe we inhabit. Yet there are moments when we feel at home here, not strangers or interlopers or resident aliens in time and space, but fellow travelers with all that is.

That sense of kinship was palpable, I think, when Sojourner rolled across the dusty Martian soil to visit a collection of rocks named Barnacle Bill, Caspar, Scooby Doo, Yogi and Boo-boo. Of course the boulders weren't truly alive, didn't really have names, or personalities, or individual identities. They weren't even cartoon characters, merely mineral formations. But personifying rocks and rivers and clouds and comets is a common (if somewhat childlike) way of expressing the personal connection we feel toward the world around us. You could even say that God is a personification of this type. Behind the word is our yearning to relate to the cosmos as a "Thou" and not merely as an "It," as a Mother and not merely as an Other.

The claim of faith, at least of my own faith, is that those feelings of companionship are not entirely misplaced. For my own cosmology rests on a fundamental belief that human beings are a part of nature. You and I have grown out of this world and are inseparable from it. Human beings have not been placed here by any supernatural power. Rather our existence is an organic expression of an evolutionary process billions of years in the making.

All of us are products of the Big Bang, giving us a truly luminous past. Thirteen billion years ago, according to the current best estimate, everything that exists erupted into being, bursting forth from a singularity smaller than a proton but containing all the matter and energy (as well as all the time and space) that would later spread across countless eons and light-years. Only the lightest elements, hydrogen and helium, were forged in the original fireball, for only the simplest structures could withstand the terrific heat of the initial blast. Every other element of our nerve and bone has been cooked inside the ovens of vanished stars many times more massive than our sun, which fused hydrogen nuclei into more helium, then used the helium as fuel to make heavier elements, until finally iron had been formed, at which point the burning stopped and the star exploded, flinging its contents into the outer reaches of space.

Those scattered remains eventually formed new stars, some with planets like our own. In our case, the iron would find its way into the hemoglobin of our blood. A similar molecule, with magnesium rather than iron at the center, became chlorophyll. Plant or animal, all life would be built of the same components — oxygen, nitrogen, hydrogen and carbon. Ninety-nine percent of the vital parts of every living organism—from blue whales to bacteria—are made of these four atoms, which have exactly the right valences for forming the delicately-balanced bonds needed to make living beings, just tight enough to provide chemical stability while still loose enough permit metabolism to take place at room temperatures. And those who share this complex, organic chemistry are the descendants of titanic energies, blown into birth by supernovae that briefly fluoresced with the light of an entire galaxy before bequeathing themselves to posterity. Our bodies and brains are the offspring of that radiant outpouring. And consciousness is a natural outgrowth of this same unfolding.

This universe we now inhabit includes roughly ten billion trillion stars, containing some 10^{80} protons and neutrons, and not one of them is extraneous or tangential; every jot is a part of the main. As astrophysicist John Gribbin explains in his book *In Search of Schrödinger's Cat*, "particles that were once together in an interaction remain in some sense parts of a single system."

Virtually everything we see and touch and feel is made up of collections of particles that have been involved in interactions with other particles right back through time, to the Big Bang in which the universe as we know it came into being. The atoms in my body are made of particles that once jostled in close proximity in the cosmic fireball with particles that are now part of a distant star, and particles that form the body of some living creature on some distant, undiscovered planet. Indeed, the particles that make up my body once jostled in close proximity and interacted with the particles that now make up your body.

We not only share a common origin, you and I, but are tethered in an ongoing network of mutuality. For the bits and pieces that rubbed shoulders once upon a time remain more intimately linked than we realize.

This is because, in modern physics, what were once considered discrete entities have begun to look more like waves on an ocean or threads in a seamless garment of creation. Shoot two quanta of radiant energy in opposite directions from a single source of light, then measure the spin of the northbound photon. No matter how far apart the two have traveled — to the ends of universe, even — the spin of the southbound counterpart will be immediately affected. Though seemingly distinct, separated by time and millions of miles, the pair remain as closely related as *here* and *there, right* and *left, up* and *down* — like the opposing poles of a magnet that appear to separate phenomena but are actually two sides of a single coin.

And that is just how closely we are related to each other and to everything else in the universe. Without much hyperbole, it could be said that our innermost thoughts and *Alpha Centauri,* the nearest star, are but varied expressions of one great energetic occurrence.

So what is it about the night sky that ignites such sensations of sublimity in the human race? Perhaps looking upward stirs a memory of who we are and where we come from. Maybe we are "remembering" in the same way the falling rain re-members its identity with the ocean, or the way a leaf re-members when it drops to the forest floor. To remember in this root sense means to "become a member" once again, to take one's place within a community or more inclusive body of life. We are naturally drawn toward the flickering stars, the creamy moonlight, the steady beacon of the planets, because they recall us to our former selves.

This point of view is obviously very different from the ancient cosmology of the Church Fathers, who looked upon the human species as sojourners or visitors in this world, destined for an otherworldly home. "Our hearts are restless," Augustine said, "until they rest in Thee." A beautiful sentiment, but for Augustine it implied that humankind would never know any real sense of peace or belonging in this world of sun and starlight. We yearn to be elsewhere, in a heavenly abode.

So for early Christians the natural world was felt to be a pale shadow of the supernal realm. Human experience was not unitary, but divided between time and eternity, body and soul, the corrupt and the imperishable.

But if a naturalistic theology diverges from the teachings of the ancient church, it is equally distinct from the mechanism of many modern scientists. For it holds that the human mind and spirit are integral aspects of the universe itself, kindled from the same magic spark that breathes life into dead equations and makes them fly. At some mysterious level, people are a match for this world. This galaxy, though just one of billions, is our native soil—not merely the cauldron for the chemicals that compose our bodies, but also the cradle of our imagining. And this means that the feelings of awe and reverence and wonder we feel when we gaze upward and contemplate the starry night are not merely unfounded sentiments or unproven hypotheses. They are valid clues that the universe that gave us birth is not only a collection of objects, but a communion of subjects. Human beings are an infinitesimal part of an incredibly big universe, yet still a part: a microcosm of the greater whole. And if that is true, then there is indeed, as poet Robinson Jeffers said, "a great humaneness at the heart of things."

Whether or not we discover life on Mars, whether or not we ever receive the radio signals that will inform us of sentient beings on other worlds, or get a phone call from E.T., I will remain convinced that we are not alone. The odds are overwhelming that we have company here. Our galaxy alone is so big that if we tried to produce an atlas of it, giving each star one page of the book, we would need a library larger than Harvard's to hold all the volumes. At this writing, eighty-five planets have been identified outside our own solar system, and surely this is only a minuscule fraction of the total. With so many worlds, it seems inevitable that some will produce life, including beings with minds as quirky and inquisitive as our own. But the sheer number of planets, the magnitude and scale of space, also inevitably raises the question: Who are we, such fragile and ephemeral creatures, set down amid these dread immensities? My answer is that we are star dust, deeply and forever related to a beautiful and ever-changing cosmos.

Thoreau, on the banks of Walden Pond, was asked if he did not sometimes grow lonely surrounded by so much solitude. "Lonely?" he responded. "Why should I be lonely? I live in the Milky Way." We all live here in the Milky Way, of course. But what is even more remarkable is that the Milky Way—in all its brilliance and unfathomed extent—also lives in us.

ALL IS FORGIVEN, GALILEO!

It's funny when someone who is supposedly infallible has to admit a goof. So others may have enjoyed a small chuckle, like me, when the Roman Catholic Church finally decided to concede the Pope's error in condemning the work of the great astronomer Galileo Galilei. The Vatican issued an apology back in 1992, after a delay of more than 350 years. News reports recounted the familiar story of how Galileo (1564-1642) was brought to trial for teaching the heretical view, first advanced by Nicholas Copernicus, that the earth is not the center of the universe, but is only one of many planets circling the sun. Galileo's disavowal of the heliocentric system after being threatened with the rack is usually understood as an illustration of the difference between the inquisitive spirit of science and the inquisitorial methods of misguided ecclesiastics. His parting murmur to his judges, *"It still moves,"* is taken as the triumph of hard fact over pious superstition. And the long overdue reversal by the Vatican is seen as merely one in a long train of rearguard actions whereby the beleaguered defenders of faith have been forced to yield more and more terrain to the advancing armies of enlightenment.

It all makes great newspaper copy, even if it's not strictly true. For, in fact, the quarrel between Galileo and the Church was a good deal more complicated than the journalists make out. In those days, the Church was not really opposed to science or bound to a narrow interpretation of the Bible. Theologians had accepted willingly, for instance, what Magellan proved so dramatically with his circumnavigation of the globe, that the earth is round — not flat as in the book of Genesis. When experiment proved the Bible wrong, the scriptures could be reinterpreted. The question in 1633 was whether the Copernican theory of a heliocentric universe had been proven conclusively, like the shape of the earth, or whether it was merely guesswork. And as a theory, it had many weaknesses.

For one thing, it couldn't predict or account for the motion of the planets any better than the Ptolemaic system it tried to replace. This is because Copernicus imagined the planets moved about the sun in perfect circles, and even after Kepler showed planetary motion to take the form of an ellipse, Galileo persisted in clinging to circular motion. It took a jerry-rigged system of circles within circles, rolling backward and forward, to explain the way the planets appeared to process through the firmament. There were other, competing theories that seemed to explain the workings of the heavens as well or better, like the Earth-centered universe proposed by the astronomer Tycho Brahé (1546-1601). And what Galileo regarded as conclusive proof of his ideas was really no proof at all. He thought the Earth's revolution around the sun, combined with its daily rotation, to be the reason for the tides. Galileo couldn't show how this could produce more than one tide each day, and since every sailor knows there are two, he rationalized the discrepancy as due to irregularities on the bottom of the sea. Still, Galileo considered this the clinching argument for Copernicanism, when of course it's the moon's gravity, not the earth's orbit about the sun, that accounts for the twice-daily rise and fall in sea level. So there were many good reasons why Christopher Clavius and the other Vatican astronomers were reluctant to accept Galileo's claims as absolute. They not only contradicted church teaching, but violated the common sense of humankind which tells us plainly that the Earth stands still while the sun, moon and other celestial bodies travel through the sky.

Nonetheless, it was Galileo who finally prevailed and who forever changed our understanding of our own place in the cosmos. After Galileo discovered the moons of Jupiter, even his detractors had to admit that not everything revolves around the Earth, and after his telescope began to reveal thousands of stars not even visible to the naked eye, most people had to wonder whether all these worlds had been created simply for the enjoyment of humankind. The privileged position that *Homo sapiens* had occupied in the universe of faith was no longer plausible.

What's more, Galileo's studies of falling objects and projectiles laid the basis for the fundamental laws of motion that seemed to drain the world of purpose. In the classical and medieval worldview drawn from Aristotle, objects moved because they were endowed with an "entelechy" or inborn aim that directed them toward a point of harmony or completion. Rain fell, for instance, because water's *raison d'etre* was to nourish the soil. Each thing moved naturally toward its divinely appointed goal. But Galileo showed motion to be governed by simple laws of physics. It had been asked, for example, how it was possible for the Earth to spin on its axis without knocking people off their feet, or leaving a trail of clouds and other unattached flotsam in its wake. In answering the question, Galileo showed that a stone dropped from the top of a ship's mast would not be left behind the speeding vessel, but carried along, because it shared the ship's momentum. By analogy, clouds, people and other terrestrial creatures shared the earth's impetus, and were carried along with *terra firma* in its travels. Things in motion tended to stay in motion. So while it would remain for Newton to formalize the law of inertia, Galileo demonstrated that no divine assistance was needed to keep the planets on their courses, and no "final cause" or purpose was needed to explain why objects moved through space.

The ultimate result was the modern understanding of cosmology in which the human race inhabits one small planet, circling a medium-sized star, which is only one of about one hundred billion stars in the Milky Way galaxy. Since the 1920s, astronomers have also realized that this galaxy is in turn only one of about a trillion galaxies in the visible universe — not even our pretty spiral has any special distinction amid its myriad cousins. And all of those countless galaxies are hurtling through space for no apparent purpose, racing away from one another at fantastic speeds with no destination or end in sight. For years, it was believed the expansion must be slowing down, as gravity slowly tightened its grip. But the latest findings indicate that the expansion rate may be speeding up — perhaps propelled by an enigmatic "dark energy" that no one seems to fully understand. If so, then we live on an insignificant mote of dust in a vast cosmos that is accelerating rapidly, but going nowhere fast.

Or do we? Einstein once said the most important question that could be asked is whether we live in a friendly universe, and there are many physicists today who think the answer is affirmative. They believe that the universe may, after all, be designed for life, and that human beings are not mere ephemera in sidereal time but have an important role to play in cosmic evolution. Although these thinkers are a decided minority among their colleagues, they include some of the finest minds in science, like the mathematical physicist Freeman Dyson, of Princeton's legendary Institute for Advanced Study, and the astrophysicist John Wheeler, who wrote what is still the basic textbook on gravitation and in the process pioneered the concept of Black Holes. Their theories are not proven, any more than Galileo's theories were proven at the time of his trial. But if they are right, there is an "anthropic principle" built into our universe: a basic law that favors and maybe even requires the evolution of conscious life.

"The more I examine the universe and study the details of its architecture, the more evidence I find that the universe in some sense must have known we were coming," says Dyson in his book *Disturbing the Universe*. One of the supreme achievements of modern physics, he notes, has been the discovery of certain "constants of nature." Such quantities as the speed of light and the ratio between the mass of the proton and electron, when taken together, have determined the major physical features of our universe, from its size and chemical composition to the formation of stars and comets. These "constants of nature" are pure numbers. They were present at the very creation, and if their values had been only slightly different, the cosmos would have taken a radically alien shape. The question arises, then, why these physical constants have their assigned numerical values and no other. The answer Dyson gives is that these numbers were required to produce life. If the relation between the electromagnetic and the nuclear force were only slightly different, for example, carbon atoms could never have formed, and life, including human physicists, would not have evolved.

There are not too many of these constants. There are only four physical forces (gravitation, electromagnetism, the strong nuclear force and weak nuclear force) and four kinds of stable particles (protons, neutrons, electrons and neutrinos). But there are wide variations in the mass of these particles and in the way the forces interact, leading to a huge number of hypothetical combinations in their relations with each other. Lee Smolin, who teaches at the Center for Gravitational Physics and Geometry, decided to figure the odds of arriving at parameters that could produce a universe hospitable to the formation of stars. As it turns out, there are innumerable combinations that conjure up cold, dark worlds, but extremely few that have the trick of creating any light or warmth. The chances of producing incandescent stellar objects of the kind we depend on to illuminate our Earth are, in round numbers, 1 in 10^{229} (a numeral that would be written with a one, followed by 229 zeros), a figure astronomically larger than the estimated number of atoms in the known universe. Not even Las Vegas stacks the deck that unfavorably. "Luck will certainly not do here," Smolin writes of his calculations. "We need some rational explanation of how something this unlikely turned out to be the case."

Even the fact that space has three dimensions, rather than four or more, has profound significance. The General Theory of Relativity conceives of gravity in terms of the curvature of space, according to the famous aphorism that "matter tells space how to bend, space tells matter how to move." One implication is that the pull of gravity depends on the dimensionality of space. In three dimensions, that pull is proportional to the inverse square of the distance between two objects, whereas in four-dimensional space, gravity would be proportional to the inverse cube of the distance. But no stable orbits would be possible in a universe where an inverse cube rule applied. The moon would fall into the Earth, Earth would cascade into the sun at the least provocation.* So despite science fiction writers' penchant for marauding villains and enlightened warriors who live in the *nth* dimension, no such characters are likely to show up outside the pages of potboiler novels. Fortunately or unfortunately, the only kind of universe likely to produce such colorful figures is precisely the kind we happen to live in.

There were many curious coincidences like these in the creation of the world. Stephen Hawking points out that "If the rate of expansion one second after the Big Bang had been smaller by even one part in a hundred thousand million it would have recollapsed before it reached its present size." Similarly, if the rate had been a tiny fraction higher, the universe would have expanded too rapidly for stars or planets to condense out of the dust. Says Hawking, "The odds against a universe like ours emerging out of something like the Big Bang are enormous. I think there are clearly religious implications."

---

* While string theory does propose the existence of spatial dimensions not visible to the naked eye, these are "curled up" into loops measuring less than a billionth of a billionth of a meter and so do not register on the scale where they might affect stars or planets.

John Wheeler shares that assessment, asking us to imagine a world in which "one or another of the fundamental dimensionless constants of physics is altered by a few percent one way or another." He wryly notes that we can't imagine it, since if it were so, none of us would be here to do the imagining. "It is not only that we are adapted to the universe," he concludes. "The universe is also adapted to us."

One could go even farther to say that conscious life is needed to bring the world into being. At least, that's one conclusion Wheeler draws from modern quantum theory. According to the most common interpretation of quantum mechanics (the so-called Copenhagen version), events at the subatomic level are nothing more than waves of probability until an act of observation collapses the wave into actual particles with position, velocity and all the other accoutrements of reality. And it follows that the universe could never have gotten started, unless at some point in its development it was going to produce observers to see it all happen. If quantum theory is correct, mind is not just an afterthought in the cosmos, but an essential ingredient in the creation of the world. In Wheeler's words, we live in a "participatory universe," which implies that human beings are something more than mere spectators enjoying the show. In a curious way, we also appear to be actors in the play and authors of the script.

Wheeler calls his theory "genesis by observership." He conjectures that not all "observers" need be self-aware. A piece of mica, for instance, might record the trace of a high-energy particle with a trail of disrupted atoms; you don't necessarily need a scientist or Geiger counter to do the job. But people are at least part of the process by which the phantasmagoric clouds of quantum uncertainty take on actual existence.

This means that we are part of an unfinished creation, one that is being built even as we watch. And it is not only the present or the future that are under construction, but also the past. For as we look into the depths of time and space—observing the light that left quasars that were burning billions of years ago—we are helping to shape the configuration of the early universe itself. What was packed into the "initial singularity" was not only an astounding compression of matter and energy but also a nearly infinite array of possible universes. And which of numerous quantum trajectories the cosmos finally decides to take is based partly on our present observations.

None of this is easy to believe—at least for me. It offends common sense, just as Galileo's theories violated the common sense of his contemporaries 350 years ago. How could such small and transitory beings as us figure in the imponderable stretches of time and space?

Accepting change is always difficult, but changing cos-
mologies is colossally hard. I grew up, for instance,
learning that atoms were like miniature solar systems
and that molecules looked like tinker toys. Never mind if
such models were oversimplified or outdated—the science I absorbed from "Mr. Wizard" on TV had a *gosh-
and-gee-whiz* aura of factuality. And one of the "facts" I
learned along the way was that we human beings are
merely accidents in the universe, cosmic flukes who have
no real reason for being here. Professor Smolin, who is on
the physics faculty at Pennsylvania State University, suggests that my own education was not so unusual in this
regard. Frustrated that he was unable to impart his own
love of science to his pupils, he finally realized that
physics is the only subject in the university curriculum
where first-year students rarely get beyond what was
known in 1900. And young people don't like what they
are learning because, as Smolin says, "there is no place
for life in the Newtonian universe," leaving students
emotionally disengaged. The world is a machine, plain
and simple; there is zero tolerance for sentiment or
human aspiration. And this is presented as the "scientific" way of looking at things. Not believing this means
risking ridicule—like declaring you don't believe the
earth is round (it's actually oblate, or slightly pumpkin-
shaped). Not to believe it means risking the accusation of

being woolly-minded or impractical, condemned as a fanatic in the court of public opinion.

But that court has no power to punish or imprison. It cannot confine our bodies or our minds. And while Galileo's battle with the Church broke new ground for the seventeenth century, physicists of the present day are opening the possibility that science can once again be the ally of religion rather than its enemy. We can, if we so choose, believe that the world does have meaning. While we can no longer hold that the earth is at the center of universe, we can still affirm that each one of us is a center of consciousness and creativity, with a vital part to play in the story of creation. We can have faith that although we are indeed very small and the cosmos is very big, we are not totally inconsequential, but have an important purpose within the grand design.

But anyone who has ever admired a spider's silken web or the spiral shell of a nautilus knows that design does not necessarily imply a Designer. And the anthropic principle does not suggest that nature's felicitous engineering is necessarily the product of an all-powerful deity. The theory is not a throwback to the idea of an omniscient overlord who resides outside of space and beyond time, setting the world in motion, adjusting and tinkering with its laws. Nor is it related to the notion of "Intelligent Design," which is merely that same tired, tinkering old Providence masquerading in more modern guise. Rather, the proposed principle holds that a disposition toward life resides within nature itself—including human nature. The God who made the world in six days might presumably have worked for three days or four and then knocked off for lunch—with day and night, oceans and dry land completed, but not a single living creature to witness the spectacle of it all. The drama of creation would then have played to an empty theater, something the anthropic principle strictly contradicts.

God, in the traditional understanding, is fully self-contained and needs nothing from his relationship with others. Scholastic philosophy in the High Middle Ages called this the doctrine of God's *aseity*. As opposed to all created beings, who were caused and contingent, the divine essence was understood as uncaused and non-dependent on any outside force. "God needs nothing, asks nothing, and demands nothing, like the stars," writes Annie Dillard, echoing this view. "You do not have to sit outside in the dark. If, however, you want to look at the stars, you will find that darkness is necessary. But the stars neither require nor demand it." Yet perhaps the stars need someone to gaze on them, after all. For if we accept the premise of a "participatory universe," observers are an indispensable element in the instigation of things. The Creator could not work at all without "creatures" to assist in the world's gestation. And Andrei Linde, a physicist at Stanford, takes Wheeler one step farther when he says those creatures also need to be intelligent:

> *We are together, the universe and us. The moment you say that the universe exists without any observers, I cannot make any sense out of that. I cannot imagine a consistent theory of everything that ignores conscious-ness. A recording device cannot play the role of an observer, because who will read what is written on the recording device? In order for us to see that something happens, and say to one another that something hap-pens, you need to have a universe, you need to have a recording device, and you need to have us.*

If Linde is right, a piece of mica will not do. Strange as it may seem, the world could not get by without us.

Inevitably, some are skeptical—and skepticism is a good instinct in both science and theology. Maybe other worlds exist where no life is viable—worlds of eight spa-tial dimensions, or where basic forces like electromagnet-ism have quite different values. Is our nurturing, inviting universe just part of a larger multiverse—one bright, shining exception among a vast array of failures, cre-ations that were misbegotten or stillborn? Could a strange and inhospitable cosmos be emerging right now in the lidless crevasse of some black hole, popping out at right angles to our own spacetime? While some scientists do speculate as much, such theories can probably never be tested, since these drab, lifeless realms would presumably exist in a geometry perpendicular to ours—forever inaccessible to direct investigation.

In the one universe we are familiar with, life seems far from coincidental. The fossil record here on Earth stretches back almost four billion years—very nearly as old as the planet itself. As soon as carbon and other necessary elements had been prepared in the bellies of the stars, and as soon as the surface of our own globe had hardened and cooled slightly, life had its advent. Judging from the time scale involved, this was no afterthought. There was no long period of dithering or waiting around for a fortuitous series of lucky accidents to transpire. Back in the 1950s, Stanley Miller and Harold Urey at the University of Chicago carried out a famous experiment where they flashed an electric spark through a container of ammonia, methane, hydrogen and water, presumed to be the main ingredients of Earth's early atmosphere. Amino acids—the building blocks for proteins—were formed, suggesting that life might have originated when lightening struck the tidal pool of some inert, antediluvian ocean, creating "primordial soup" where the first prokaryotic cells could arise. But now we know that amino acids can be found in the clouds of interstellar space and are widely dispersed throughout the cosmos. So there was no need for the first organism to bide its time, waiting for a thunderbolt to strike. Life happened quickly, as soon as conditions were right. It appears to be what the universe was intending from the very inception.

The anthropic principle will never satisfy those who long for the certainties of yesteryear. Indeed, it raises as many questions as it answers. How can present-day observations affect what happened in the long-ago past? What exactly is this conundrum called time? (One wag said that "time is God's way of keeping everything from happening at once.") Just how did the universe manage to see us coming? Or was it dolphins, rather than people, for which our wet, watery world was especially designed and adapted? (The anthropic principle might better be called the "biotic theorem," for although *anthropos* is the Greek word for *human*, there is nothing to suggest that the constants of nature particularly favor *Homo sapiens* over other forms of life.) But questions are less detriments to religious belief than aids to wonder. And whether or not the anthropic principle can ever be verified, our ideas of God will never be the same again. For ever since Galileo, everything is awhirl. There are no fixed points, in heaven or on earth. Like the cosmos itself, faith expands. The spirit is not stationary. *It moves.*

A BRIEF HISTORY OF STUFF

A dozen years ago, the physicist Stephen Hawking wrote a best-selling book titled *A Brief History of Time*. It spent a record 200 weeks on the London *Sunday Times* bestseller list and sold ten million copies in thirty languages around the world. Like lots of other people, I bought the book and tried to read it without really being able to understand the whole thing.

I suspect that part of the book's popularity sprang from the author's rather tragic biography. Diagnosed with amyotrophic lateral sclerosis as a student at Oxford, Hawking has become the living paradox of fiery intellect trapped within a useless body. And perhaps part of the public's fascination with Hawking springs as well from the manner in which his personal predicament mimics our more general dilemma. For if Hawking has found himself a captive or prisoner to his own body, all of us living at the opening of the twenty-first century could be described as strangers in a strange land, our minds and spirits held hostage by a physical universe that seems increasingly alien, inhospitable or even hostile to our own humanity.

Like some slow-growing disease, the ideology of materialism has gradually infected the scientific worldview and then popular culture, slowly but surely taking over the senses, one by one. As defined by the dictionary, materialism is "the philosophic doctrine that matter is the only reality and that everything in the world, including thought, will and feeling, can be explained in terms of matter alone." Materialism informs us that the world is composed of senseless "stuff," where blind mechanical forces hold sway. Life, love, freedom and spirit are merely illusions, in this view, that can be reduced through rigorous analysis to combinations of electrochemical interactions. What can't be torn down to a material substrate doesn't really exist, and this foundation is at bottom pretty poor and disappointing: unfeeling, uncaring and impersonal in nature.

Existence in a purely material world is very much like existence in a body crippled by ALS, characterized by an almost impossible sense of helplessness and futility. As biologist Richard Dawkins, one of the leading proponents of this view, puts it, "In a universe of blind physical forces . . . some people are going to get hurt, and other people are going to get lucky, and you won't find any rhyme or reason in it, nor any justice. The universe that we observe has precisely the properties we should expect if there is, at bottom, no design, no purpose, no evil, and no good, nothing but blind, pitiless indifference." And if that truly is an accurate description of our world, then all of us are in pretty much the same position as Mr. Hawking, able to understand our situation perfectly, but incapable of lifting a finger to do anything about it.

Materialism robs us of our vitality and saps the will to change. And it's hard to imagine anyone crawling into such a mental straightjacket voluntarily. Naturally, it didn't happen all at once. The process began with the Copernican revolution as science addressed the question of *where we are*. Human beings learned that they were living in a universe much larger than previously supposed, but hardly one in which our kind held any special place or privileged position. In the nineteenth century came the Darwinian revolution, which examined the question of *how we got here*. The longstanding mystery of the origin of species yielded to explanations based upon chance and necessity. Finally, materialism invaded the inner citadel of personality—the question of *who we are*—as within the twentieth century advances in genetics and molecular biology seemed to unlock the ultimate secret of mind and consciousness itself.

Not too long ago, it was still possible to believe that each person possessed an eternal soul, a divine spark, a sacred essence. The individual was seen as a moral agent and creative force within the unfolding drama of history, but breakthroughs in genetics have seemingly reduced ingenuity and daring, heroism and sacrifice, to nothing more than the chance combinations of chromosomes. As Francis Crick, the discoverer of DNA, has written, "the astonishing hypothesis is that 'you,' your joys and your sorrows, your memories and your ambitions, your sense of personal identity and free will, are in fact no more than the behavior of a vast assembly of nerve cells and their associated molecules." Philosopher of science Daniel Dennett agrees that "You are made of robots—or what comes to the same thing, a collection of trillions of macromolecular machines." Goodbye gallantry. Aloha to praise and blame. Farewell to the quaint notion that you have a hand in your own destiny, or a purpose for being here that it's your job to discover and fulfill. For in this brave new world, you're nothing but the pawn and play-thing of your genes.

This story has often been told in terms that have become familiar to all of us as the contest between sci-ence and religion, enlightenment and progress versus ignorance and reaction. And yet, ironically, the ideology of materialism is more an outgrowth of ancient mythology than of modern experimentation. Its roots actually lie in the creation narrative of the Hebrew Bible and the cosmology of the Greeks. I'm sure most readers are familiar with Genesis, where God brings the world into being. Sunbeam and moonlight, earth and sky, flowering plants and animals appear at the divine command. God then molds Adam's frame out of mud, as a potter shapes a vessel, and breathes into the inert form, filling the first human with the divine gift, the animating principle of awareness and life. And the primordial stuff that God employs to make the world, the raw materials for the six days that follow, are rendered in Hebrew as *tohu va bohu*, which means undifferentiated chaos. Later, Christian theologians would develop the doctrine of *creatio ex nilhilo*, or "creation out of nothing." But whether God creates the world out of the void or works in the beginning with some primal gooey mess, there is a clear and absolute division between matter and spirit, the Creator and the creation. And the physical world apart from God, the realm of nature—of tangible reality and everyday objects—is empty of any special significance or interesting properties that might give stuff its own independent value. In the Great Chain of Being—one of the guiding images of the High Middle Ages—the world was pictured as a hierarchy of goodness: God at the top, with angels and other disembodied beings directly underneath, followed by men and women and then animals, with rocks and dirt and other seemingly worthless muck at the bottom. Matter, whatever else it might be, was considered distinctly fifth-rate, shoddy merchandise.

The idea of the Great Chain owed as much to the Greeks as to the Jews. For Plato and Aristotle both taught that this earthly sphere is a very sad and sorry copy of a much better and finer world, a world that Plato located in the realm of ideas and Aristotle placed in the celestial rotations of the heavens. You might say that for Aristotle, the universe was divided into first class and steerage, for the *hoi polloi*. The upper decks were supposedly made of transparent crystal. But other Greek philosophers speculated as to what this lower, more mundane world might be made of. Thales said everything was made of water. Others said fire. Democritus held a theory that everything was made of atoms, invisible particles so small they were incapable of any further subdivision, constantly colliding in their ceaseless motion and occasionally combining into larger structures when they happened to have interlocking shapes. And of course, modern materialism owes a major debt to Democritus. For what happened is that as traditional concepts of God slowly lost their credibility, and as the antique physics and metaphysics of Plato and Aristotle also faded into obscurity — for there is no ethereal plane of crystal spheres or rational perfection to be found beyond the moon's orbit—what we were left with was an archaic view of matter. What is the world made of? Unthinking, worthless muck. Particles aimlessly bouncing about and sometimes assuming accidental patterns. Brainless forces and lifeless clods of fourth-rate junk. Now notice that these are not the answers given by contemporary research. They are mythological, almost superstitious answers that took shape thousands of years ago, but that linger on as the faith statements of many devout materialists.

What is matter? The philosopher Bertrand Russell (1872–1970) says that even as a child, he was enamored of such big questions. But his parents were not very encouraging. He asked them, "What is matter?" To which they replied, "Never mind." He then asked, "What is mind?" To which his parents responded, "No matter." And yet twentieth-century physics suggests that mind and matter are very much intertwined, both on the scale of the very large and the infinitesimally tiny. As an ideology, materialism has been discredited. Why would anyone take seriously the arguments of a proponent of this position, whose words by his own admission are nothing more than the empty echoes of senseless, brute forces at work—full of sound and fury but (like the rest of the universe) signifying nothing? As science, materialism has more to do with the physics of the nineteenth century—when Lord Kelvin declared that he could build a three-dimensional model of anything he studied—than with the ten dimensions of modern string theory.

A contemporary particle physicist might admit that we haven't come too far from the summary given by Ernest Rutherford (1871–1937), who first discovered the atomic nucleus almost a hundred years ago. I recall reading somewhere that when asked to describe his great discovery, he replied to the effect that, "Something—we don't know what—is doing something—we don't know how." And that sense of bafflement has only increased as the subatomic world has revealed entities like muons and mesons, which seem to proliferate faster than gerbils, and as even subatomic particles have been torn down into quarks and quarks into strings, which are mere one-dimensional loops of vibrating energy.

At first sight, the universe appears to be made of a whole lot of nothing. Take away the empty space, and the average human being would be reduced to a speck roughly the same size as a typical grain of sand. That same grain of sand from the seashore, we are now told, holds enough energy to drive a battleship across the ocean. And the ship and the sea itself are composed almost entirely of empty spaces between the atoms, which themselves have a fairly deserted look about them. If you picture a single atom magnified to the size of Yankee Stadium, the electrons would then hover like a cloud of gnats above and around the ballpark, higher and farther away than any home run Hank Aaron ever hit, while the nucleus, smaller than a baseball, sits all by its lonesome in the center field; everything in between is vacant, empty space.

"Empty space" is not what it used to be, however. Physicists now tell us that what we formerly called a vacuum is actually sizzling with all kinds of energy fields, and that those fields are continually giving birth to a variety of "virtual particles" that pop into existence and then disappear again in something less than a trillionth of a nanosecond. Inside the proton, we are informed, swarms of these virtual particles—quarks, gluons, pairs of electrons and anti-electrons and other ultra-miniature entities—come and go each moment, a little like an electrical storm inside an unimaginably small bottle. But the deeper you dig, the more these tiny bodies tend to smear out into mere nothingness, and the closer their electrical charges fall toward zero, resembling one comedian's description of a dull midwestern city: "There's no *there* there." Unless a lot of nothing adds up to something, where then does the proton acquire its substantiality? Says Frank Wilczek, who helped craft the theory of quantum chromodynamics that describes this will o' the wisp world, "If you really study the equations, it gets almost mystical."

I don't think you have to understand all the details to grasp that physics is formulating a very different answer to the question, "What is the world made of?" Matter, perhaps, but matter is much more curious and potent stuff than either the Greeks or Hebrews dreamed. I think it's not going too far to suggest that we need an entirely new creation story. For the Big Bang scenario tells us when it all started — thirteen billion years ago, more or less — and how it all started — in a sudden rocketing blast whose dim echo we can still hear with our radio telescopes, the so-called background radiation that fills the sky in every direction at 2.73 degrees above absolute zero — but it doesn't tell us enough about who or what was present at the creation.

"Who or what" may be a loaded pairing of pronouns. But if mind and matter really do coexist and co-evolve within our cosmos, then I think it's fair to say that some form of intelligence and subjectivity was incipient even in the original fireball. Einstein, after all, remarked that the most incomprehensible thing about our universe is that it seems so comprehensible. Physicist Eugene Wigner (1902–1995) put it slightly differently, commenting on the "unreasonable effectiveness of mathematics." Why should formulae scribbled in chalk on a blackboard be able to tell us anything about what happened billions of years ago, in the first three minutes? Yet the odd fact remains that beneath the quarks and before the strings, there are and always were the equations so oddly transparent to the human mind. And in their search for the ultimate equations—the so-called "theory of everything"—physicists and mathematicians are guided not only by the hard data they can gather from their cyclotrons and cloud chambers. They are also guided by a much softer feel for solutions that satisfy an aesthetic sense, a solution that will be beautiful or elegant.

Not every beautiful story need be true, of course. And many charming hypotheses turn out to be invalid. Nor is elegance the same as being simple or easy to understand. There is a famous story about two outstanding scientists from the twentieth century, Niels Bohr (1885-1962) and Werner Heisenberg (1901-1976). Both were pioneers in the creation of quantum theory, working in uncharted territory. Once Heisenberg proposed an idea to Bohr, and after studying it for a while Bohr responded, "It isn't crazy enough to be true." Later Bohr remarked, "Great innovations inevitably appear muddled, confusing and incomplete, only half understood by their discoverers and a mystery to everyone else. There is no hope for any speculation that does not look absurd at first glance." Though Tertullian, a theologian from the second century of the Christian era, might agree ("I believe because it is absurd," he famously asserted), theories that are merely implausible or bizarre do not necessarily have that *je ne sais quoi*. But the stories that are most deeply and enduringly true must also be elegant, at least if we can believe the physicists.

Elegance as scientists use the term is a special trait, like genius in art or passion in music. It's a quality that is undeniably real, though impossible to quantify or measure. A clergy friend of mine who studied engineering in his younger years says he had the briefest glimpse of it, when a window of clarity opened into Maxwell's equations, the rules that govern the diffusion of electromagnetic radiation—from the visible spectrum to gamma rays and radio at either end. The mathematics momentarily came to life for him, as if the shaped notes on a musical staff suddenly acquired voices and the score began to sing. The window closed again, unfortunately, and my friend went on to enter the ministry. But at least for an instant, he knew that science could offer a vision every bit as breathtaking as that available through religious inspiration. Maxwell had spoken to him, saying, "Let there be light!" For those who have been to the mathematical mountaintop, elegance is palpable. And whoever did the math or laid out the architect's drawings for the universe seems to have had a gift for elegance in abundance. For we seem to inhabit a universe that is not only intelligible, but constructed with soul-satisfying grace. And that is why we need a new accounting of our origins today or, if you will, a brief history of stuff.

The ancient myths of the Hebrews and the Greeks are indeed lovely and suggestive of many profound insights, but not literally true, and so not able to fully orient us in time or space. The creation narrative outlined by astrophysics is likewise grand and compelling, and perhaps stays closer to the facts, but too often leaves us cold and feeling adrift in a world that dwarfs human emotion. As theologian Thomas Berry writes, "The pathos in our own situation is that our secular society does not see the numinous quality or the deeper psychic powers associated with its own story, while the religious society rejects the story because it is presented only in its physical aspect." Assisted by physicist Brian Swimme, Father Berry has called for a New Story that can again acquaint the human race with its own origins and destiny, and in the environmental awareness stirring today, he senses that story announcing itself to the current generation:

If the dynamics of the universe from the beginning shaped the course of the heavens, lighted the sun and formed the earth, if this same dynamism brought forth the continents and seas and atmosphere, if it awakened life in the primordial cell and then brought into being the unnumbered variety of living beings, and finally brought us into being and guided us safely through the turbulent centuries, there is reason to believe that this same guiding process is precisely what has awakened in us our present understanding of ourselves and our relation to this stupendous process.

According to the New Story, this is our reason for being—to bring the cosmos to self-realization. Nobel laureate George Wald (1906–1997) put it in terms anyone can understand: "It would be a poor thing to be an atom in a universe without physicists. And physicists are made of atoms. A physicist is the atom's way of knowing about atoms." The universe, it could be said, exists to celebrate itself and revel in its own beauty. And if the human race is one facet of the cosmos growing toward awareness of itself, our purpose must surely be to preserve and perpetuate our world as well as to study it, not to despoil or destroy what has taken so long to produce. We must pass on the book of nature—whose text we have only recently begun to decipher—intact for posterity. For in understanding the universe that is our home, humankind has finally begun to fulfill the ancient dictum: "Know thy (larger) self."

I am not the one to flesh out this new creation epic, but I will venture that our new story needs to be both poetic and prosaic, appealing to the heart as well as the head. It needs to provide a unified account of the natural world, without reference to any other, supernatural domains. The universe is *wholly* material. But the universe, I believe, is also *holy* material, meaning that a new view of matter will entail a fresh understanding of God, as well. The Creator can no longer be envisioned as entirely separate from the creation—an Unmoved Mover or transcendent first principle. For whatever the world is made of, stuff appears to contain a generative and self-organizing principle.

Would it be going too far to speculate that the universe came into existence because, at some preconscious level, it chose to exist? That along with necessity and determinism, will and freedom need to be taken into account in any explanation of cosmic origins? Perhaps the universe came to be for the same reason I am now writing this book—out of a mixture of adventuresomeness and desire rather than due to any ironclad strictures of causality. And perhaps the universe will end the way this sentence ends—constrained by its opening clause and the rules of grammar (as well as the laws of thermodynamics), but otherwise free to finish off with any number of unexpected conclusions(!)

That would be consistent with what we know about reality at the quantum scale, where probability and uncertainty rule the roost. In Peter Parnell's play *QED*, which stands for *quantum electrodynamics* and which is based on the life of physicist Richard Feynman (1918–1988), the actor who plays the renowned scientist looks out at the audience through a pane of glass:

> *Take the surface of glass. You see me because light is coming through the glass and hitting my face, but you also see yourself because some of the light is reflecting back. At this angle, for every 100 photons hitting the glass, 96 go through the glass and 4 hit the glass and go back to you. How does any individual photon make up its mind which way to go?*

Even physicists will ask why a photon makes up its mind or "chooses" to manifest in one location rather than another, careful to bracket the word *chooses* in quotation marks, but lacking any better lingo than the language of choice and volition to describe what's going on.

An indwelling tendency toward self-expression might also explain why the world is so hauntingly beautiful. Creation is not a minimalist enterprise. From the gemlike symmetries of the sub-atomic realm to the brilliant flash of a peacock's tail, to the cadences of Bach and Mozart, being exercises a preferential option for the solution with verve.

And so all those people who bought Stephen Hawking's book understood something important, even if they didn't comprehend the entire argument. They were drawn to a man, not to an abstraction. And in the kind of universe I believe we inhabit, people are real as well as particles. Hawking is important for *who* he is, as well as for *what* he's written. Sympathy and compassion do count for something, along with hope and courage. These virtues have ontological standing, just as much as neutrinos, which scientists tell us may or may not have mass, but do have speed and get where they want to go. And thus we come to the final question: What is matter? What is the world made of? What is the nature of existence at its irreducible core? Some say "never mind," but I answer, "God knows."

GAIA AND THE GREAT MOTHER

When I was growing up, there was a song popular at hootenannies and sing-alongs, based on the tune *"Gimme That Old Time Religion."* One slightly irreverent verse began:

6

> *I will worship Aphrodite*
> *In her silk and satin nightie.*
> *She is beautiful but flighty.*
> *That's good enough for me!*

That was about as close to goddess worship as most of us got back then. But that was before the women's movement raised our awareness about "that old time religion." It was before Merlin Stone's *When God Was a Woman*, before Naomi Goldenberg's *The Changing of the Gods*, before Charlene Spretnak's *Lost Goddesses of Early Greece*, and before Riane Eisler's *The Chalice and the Blade*. A generation of research has changed our thinking, so that the goddess is no longer just an excuse for silly songs. Increasingly, she is the subject of serious study and reflection.

That "old time religion," say anthropologists like Marija Gimbutas, was the cult of the Great Mother, which dates back to paleolithic times and spread from the Mediterranean to the Pacific. Our early human ancestors left her image in their caves and campsites, and her clay figurines have been unearthed in archeological sites in Turkey, Europe and the Near East. Ever fertile and nurturing, she was revered as the source of life. For she was the goddess of the earth itself. It was her power that quickened the seed and enriched the soil. Out of her womb the creatures of land and sea came to birth. Her seasons and festivals were the cycles of the moon and the revolutions of solstice and equinox through which life was constantly renewed. Many believe this was the fabled "golden age" when women and men lived in peace, with each other and with nature.

Other scholars dispute this reading of the past. Cynthia Eller, in *The Myth of Matriarchal Prehistory*, argues that the widespread dispersal of fertility totems does not prove that paleolithic peoples were any less violent or hierarchical than those of later times, or that real women enjoyed any special respect within their cultures. Despite the "Venus of Willendorf," there is no firm evidence that matriarchy prevailed in those distant times, nor do the varied images unearthed prove that the goddess was held in higher esteem than other male divinities. Feminists and eco-feminists who call for a new ethic of equality and compassion in our relations with the Earth should not pin all their hopes on re-creating a vanished paradise that may never have existed.

Still, it seems fair to say that many ancient civilizations did picture the sacred in feminine form. The Greeks called her Gaia. It was she who gave birth to the other deities of the Olympian pantheon. In a Homeric hymn, her goodness is celebrated:

> *Gaia, mother of all I sing, oldest of gods.*
> *Firm of foundation, who feeds all creatures*
> *   living on earth.*
> *As many as move on the radiant land*
> *   and swim in the sea,*
> *And fly through the air — all these does she feed*
> *   with her bounty.*
> *Mistress, from you come our fine children*
> *   and bountiful harvest:*
> *Yours is the power to give mortals life*
> *   and to take it away.*

In the congregation I currently serve, we sing a hymn with much the same message, to a tune from the old Genevan psalter: "Earth shall be fair, and all her people one." Perhaps the best way to think about this language, and about Gaia too, is as an evocation of the future, rather than the past—not a description of what has been, but of what should be. One day, people will know the earth as holy and all creatures as sacred. The creative power that enlivens our universe will then be as close and accessible as a mother to her child.

Today Gaia is struggling to be born, not only as a spiritual reality but as an experimental hypothesis leading to a revised understanding of our evolution on the planet. *Gaia: A New Look at Life on Earth* is the title of James Lovelock's groundbreaking book, published by Oxford University Press in 1979, which clothed the ancient belief that the earth is a living being in modern scientific dress. The idea behind it germinated through Lovelock's work with NASA and the Jet Propulsion Laboratory when he was part of a research team charged with exploring the possible existence of life on Mars.

Early on, Lovelock realized that the Viking spacecraft being prepared to touch down and sample the Martian soil would find a barren and mostly lifeless landscape. He reasoned that life in any form exists in dynamic interaction with its environment, as currents of water and air are the vital carriers of both wastes and nutrients within a living system. From the inert Martian atmosphere, Lovelock inferred that the surface of the red planet had little or no biological activity.

The realization that life affects its surrounding environment led Lovelock to the further supposition that life might actually modulate the environment to suit its own purposes. And this is the essence of the Gaia theory. It views the earth as a single organism, in which life collaborates to regulate the temperature of the oceans and the amount of oxygen in the air, much as we regulate our own body heat and maintain the balance of our own internal chemistry. Gaia brings on ice ages when the planet needs to be cooled, just as we reflexively shiver or break into a sweat if we get too hot or cold. She maintains "homeostasis," or the equilibrium necessary to keep herself vigorous and flourishing. The rocks themselves, formed through eons of sedimentation, are actively involved in the life of Gaia. And we, along with ten million other species from the manatee to the microbe, are the corpuscles and organelles within her blue-green body.

Lovelock's thesis is not entirely original. Over ninety years ago, a professor of biochemistry at Harvard named Lawrence Henderson (1878–1942) proposed something similar in a book titled *The Fitness of the Environment: An Inquiry into the Biological Significance of the Properties of*

Matter. Henderson observed that Darwin was at least half right. Through the process of natural selection, living organisms seem deftly suited to their environment. What Darwin missed, however, is that the environment itself seems propitiously adapted to life. The oceans, for instance, are extremely constant not only in their temperature, but also in alkalinity, salt content and osmotic pressure. "Certainly nowhere else where life is possible, probably no other place in the universe, except another ocean, are so many conditions so stable or so enduring," Henderson wrote. Even the regulatory devices of a modern laboratory could not keep a dynamic system in such steady state: "The only known improvement upon the ocean is the body of a higher warm-blooded mammal." Henderson mused that the laws of nature themselves appeared to be biocentric, without however suggesting any theory as to how the ocean maintained such ideal conditions. The Harvard professor was not quite ready to take the next step—to suggest the seas themselves might actually be alive.

Biologist Lewis Thomas (1913–1993) went farther. "Viewed from the distance of the moon," he wrote in his 1974 bestseller *The Lives of a Cell*, "the astonishing thing about the earth, catching the breath, is that it is alive. The photographs show the dry, pounded surface of the moon in the foreground, dead as an old bone. Aloft, floating free beneath the moist, gleaming membrane of the bright blue sky, is the rising earth, the only exuberant thing in this part of the cosmos." His comparison of azure sky to a glistening membrane was deliberate, for the layer of atmosphere that girdles the earth didn't "just happen" any more than a cell wall happens. The primitive sky was purely the product of volcanic de-gassing and close to poisonous. The precise blend of water vapor, carbon dioxide and other gases that we take for granted—two hundred million lungfuls for each of us over the course of a typical lifespan—was created of, by and for the development of living beings like ourselves. This "organic sky" is a semi-permeable barrier that both filters out harmful radiation and admits the very wavelengths needed for photosynthesis to transpire. "You could say that the breathing of oxygen into the atmosphere was the result of evolution, or you could turn it around and say that evolution was the result of oxygen," observes Thomas. "You can have it either way." But whichever way you look at it, he concludes, it is hard not to feel affection for the sky, which is as much the product of life as bread or wine.

It was years before most other scientists started to take Gaia seriously. One who supported the notion from the very beginning, however, was microbiologist Lynn Margulis. She was called "Mother Earth" by her son when she was married to astronomer Carl Sagan (he was known as "Father Star"). But more substantial reasons drew her toward belief in Gaia. An innovative thinker, and one of the youngest women ever elected to the National Academy of Sciences, it was Margulis who first proposed that chloroplasts and mitochondria, the tiny powerhouses contained within the cells of plants and animals, had their genesis as distinct bacteria who over the course of millions of years learned to live with and within the cellular structure of other beings. Symbiosis, or cooperation among living creatures for mutual benefit, seemed to her to be the primordial law of life, so it was natural to imagine that the principle might apply to the entire planet.

Others were more skeptical, if not downright incredulous. But evidence to support the hypothesis began to accumulate. It is known, for instance, that stars like our own sun tend to grow brighter and hotter over the course of their lifetime. Through the billions of years that life has inhabited our globe, the output of solar energy must have increased on the order of twenty-five to thirty percent. Yet the average temperature of the earth has remained steadily within the comfort range for life. While the precise mechanisms Gaia uses to control the thermostat are unknown, computer models show how it would be possible for living creatures to automatically adjust the "albedo," or surface coloration of the planet, to absorb or reflect heat as needed. When the American Geophysical Union met to discuss Gaia theory in 1988, it was a sign that Lovelock's theory had moved firmly into the scientific mainstream.

Most biologists still work from a reductionistic model, whereby the way to understand life is to break it down into smaller and smaller pieces. This method has produced real advances in genetics and molecular biology. But Yale biochemist Harold Morowitz explains that a new and different approach is emerging among scientists who work from a Gaian perspective.

> For this group, life is a property of a geologically active planet whose elements keep recycling under the driving forces of solar radiation and mechanical energy from processes within the mantle and core. This viewpoint has emerged from the cooperation of ecologists, geologists, meteorologists and oceanographers . . . Findings in all these fields confirm that the life of any single organism is part of a larger-scale process involving the "metabolism" of the whole earth. Continued biological activity is then a planetary property, an interrelationship of organisms, atmosphere, oceans and continents, all of which are in some sense alive.

Where life is concerned, the whole is larger than the sum of the parts, and endless dissection can become a dead end. A balanced understanding of any living entity requires knowledge of the interconnected web of which that creature is a part.

If the Gaia hypothesis is true, one implication might be that Mother Earth is much more resourceful than previously imagined. Like a living body, she has defenses against illness and powers of healing when her balance is disrupted. Some of the alarm over current threats to the environment may therefore be exaggerated or misplaced. For instance, one problem that Lovelock believes may eventually take care of itself is depletion of the ozone. It was Lovelock, by the way, who first discovered the slow accumulation of ozone-destroying chlorofluorocarbons in the upper atmosphere. He did it with his own invention, the electron capture detector, which can find trace molecules in gases in minuscule amounts of only a few parts per trillion. In 1973, he published an article in *Nature* sharing his findings, along with his opinion that at such low levels, CFCs posed no conceivable menace to the environment. Although he has since changed his mind and now agrees that the manufacture of these chemicals should be restricted, he still feels the issue has been sensationalized. Lynn Margulis has shown that life existed for a billion years on earth with no ozone shield at all. And ultraviolet radiation, Lovelock adds, is necessary for human health. While too much can cause cancer among fair-skinned people, too little leads to rickets among those with darker pigmentation. The reason Lovelock now wants to curtail production of CFCs is not because they destroy the ozone, but because they contribute to the greenhouse effect. Global warming, in his mind, presents the far greater danger to the long-term health of Gaia.

For if Gaia is a living body, with the ability to fend off disease, she is also a vulnerable being who, like any other living creature, has vital organs that are essential to her well being. And the vital organs of our planet are likely to be in the tropics. Lovelock reminds us that over the course of the millennia, the temperate latitudes of North America and Europe have been scraped clean of life many times as glaciers advanced and then retreated. Always, the plants and animals of these regions rebounded with new luxuriance. While we mourn the death of the Black Forest in Germany and worry about the effect of acid rain on New England woodlands, these ecosystems have perished before, and Gaia has adapted. It is in the equatorial belt, where life drew its first breath, and where the rapidly disappearing rain forests continue to function as lungs of earth, that we may hear the dying gasps of our planet. At current rates, the tropics will be gone—felled for lumber, slashed and burned to pasture cattle—within a century. Without these forests to draw carbon out of the air and pump water vapor back into it, we simply do not know whether Gaia can survive.

There is no discipline of geophysiology to tell us what the other vital organs of Gaia might be. Coastal seas? The phytoplankton who populate our oceans or the living tissue of the soil? Lovelock asserts that while we have many specialists who study narrow aspects of earth's biology, the need now is for nurses and general practitioners who can diagnose the symptoms and begin to treat the patient before her condition becomes critical.

The Gaia hypothesis has generated fruitful questions in science and even more interesting issues in ethics and religion. At the most basic level, it brings us back to the fundamental question of what it means to be alive. Some have objected to the concept of a living earth, pointing out that unlike other living entities, Gaia does not reproduce. Lovelock and his defenders rejoin that Gaia has no need to replicate, since she is for all practical purposes immortal. At four billion years, she is nearly one third as old as the universe itself. Like an ancient redwood, which consists of a thin layer of living tissue wrapped around an inanimate core, Gaia has a growing edge, the delicate biosphere encircling the surface of the globe—

but as with the redwood, that thin membrane may be enough to make a vital difference.

If Gaia is alive, then it raises the equally profound question, "Who are we?" *Homo sapiens* has less reason than ever to see itself as the dominant species on the planet and must become aware of the interdependence of all beings. Like the microbes Lynn Margulis studies, who spend their whole lives within the intestines of larger animals, we exist inside the body of Gaia. She sustains us, and we must do our part to sustain her. If the earth is alive, then we presumably have ethical and moral obligations toward her, as we do toward other creatures. Lovelock writes:

> *If we are "all creatures great and small," from bacteria to whales, part of Gaia, then we are all of us potentially important to her well being. We knew in our hearts that the destruction of whole ranges of other species was wrong but now we know why.*

Such wholesale destruction is wrong because life is a community, not a commodity. And we cannot damage any member of the larger body without disrupting the health of the entirety.

Water, for example, is the lifeblood of Gaia. No other substance is so critical to the sustenance of her metabolism. The hydrologic cycle drives our weather. No other compound has played a bigger role in geological evolution. And water is the principal constituent of living organisms, including the human body. Lawrence Henderson pointed out the singular physical characteristics of H_2O that render it uniquely suitable for its preeminent role. While almost every other liquid contracts on freezing, water expands; if it were otherwise, most of our world would be locked up in ice and Gaia's surface would be as intemperate as the wastes of Antarctica. (If H_2O were like other liquids, it would become denser when frozen and sink instead of floating. Masses of ice would then collect at the bottoms of lakes and oceans, impervious to melting.) As it is, wetness abounds, providing a ready solution for the transport of food, the excretion of waste and other biological activity. There are roughly 1,360,000,000 cubic kilometers of water spread across the surface of Gaia. Were the Earth's terrain totally flat, the stuff would cover the globe to a depth of two to three miles. Fresh water is only about three percent of the total, and two thirds of that is locked up in glaciers and the polar caps. Most of the remainder is deep in underground aquifers, accumulated over countless centuries of rainwater seeping through the soil. Still, nothing could be more common than water. And at the same time, nothing is more precious than the aqueous medium that forms both our internal and external environment.

Now multinational corporations like Vivendi and Suez-Lyonnaise des Eaux are pushing for the privatization of water, not only taking over municipal water supplies from Buenos Aires to Jakarta, but also working hand in hand with the World Bank and other development agencies to construct dams and aqueducts that will divert a free running resource to those who can afford to pay. Water is already a $400 billion *per annum* global business, with many economists predicting that water will be to the twenty-first century what oil was to the twentieth. The question is who will profit and who will suffer from this development. Will wetlands and their aquatic inhabitants be shortchanged when the cash register, rather than Mother Nature, determines who has access to the tap? Torrid ecosystems can be particularly delicate and may never recover once they have been deprived of moisture. Will deserts expand? Access to water for irrigation has already become a flashpoint between Palestinians and Israelis in the arid Middle East, and global politics will only heat up as aquifers there and in other parts of the world are drained faster than they can be naturally replenished. Capitalists argue that private enterprise guarantees the most efficient use of scarce commodities. But regarding water—or any other any living system—purely as a commodity subverts our relationship with nature. Gaia has her own economy and keeps her own balance sheet. The bottom line is that we cannot take more than our share without eventually suffering the consequences.

Earth does not belong to us; rather, we and all living creatures belong to the earth. But Gaia is not merely another creature. She is in an important sense our creator, the womb and matrix of all life. And this brings us inevitably to matters of theology.

When he first proposed the Gaia hypothesis, says Lovelock, he rather relished the propect of being excoriated from the pulpit—like Galileo and other scientific pioneers. Instead, he was asked to deliver a sermon at the Cathedral of St. John the Divine in New York City and shunned by his academic peers. For the spiritually inclined, Gaia has been received like a new dispensation. If our planet is alive, is she sentient as well? Is the old belief in an *anima mundi* or "world soul" about to be confirmed by modern research? Is Mother Earth a goddess who deserves adoration from her children? Lovelock and Margulis distance themselves from the religious repercussions of their theory, stressing that science is not equipped to answer questions of faith. But Lovelock does allow that "thinking of the Earth as alive makes it seem, on happy days, in the right places, as if the whole planet were celebrating a sacred ceremony."

I have that feeling, too. There are moments when I feel that I am part of a life much larger, more powerful and more ancient than my own. I sense its presence in rocks and trees, in rivers and animals, and in the rituals of birth and sex and death. I feel deeply at home in this world, and want only to preserve it forever.

The Gaia hypothesis is a scientific theory. It can be empirically tested and may someday be overthrown. In its strongest form, the theory suggests that the planet acts almost like a beehive or ant colony—a "superorganism" where every member is meticulously adapted to serve the needs of the collective. Not even Lovelock believes that. A less stringent claim, that single species can influence the global environment, has now been well established. But on whatever level Gaia can be shown to function, the hypothesis will be immensely useful if it helps us understand in more detail our own place in nature and appreciate the wonder of life itself. Hymns of praise to our earthly mother may or may not be that "old time religion." But if the Gaia hypothesis can lead us toward deeper reverence and respect for our fragile, fruitful planet, that's good enough for me!

AFTER DARWIN

Many years ago, when I was filling out applications for college, one of the forms asked me to list three books that, in my opinion, had had the most far-ranging impact on the course of history. Being a smart-aleck high school senior, I think I listed three books that I had never read before but which I felt might impress the judges, including Charles Darwin's *The Origin of Species*. I did get accepted to several colleges, which just goes to show that you can fool some of the people some of the time (especially if they happen to be Ivy League), but by that time my interests were turning away from science and toward the humanities, religion and philosophy. It wasn't until my early forties that I finally got around to reading Mr. Darwin, when I had a chance to go back to Harvard, where I'd been an undergraduate, for a semester of study as a Merrill

Fellow at the Harvard Divinity School. Maybe my interests were shifting again, for one of the most enjoyable courses I took there was Stephen Jay Gould's "History of Life," a class that my wife had taken twenty years before when she was at Radcliffe and that she assured me was not to be missed.

Having finally read *The Origin of Species*, I think I would still list it among the titles that have revolutionized human thinking. An argument could be made that it opened a whole new era: B.C. (Before Charles) and A.D. (After Darwin). But having taken the class with Professor Gould, I appreciate more of the ironies involved in Darwin's scientific contribution. One irony: in spite of its epochal nature, Darwin's work has to be one of the most boring volumes ever written, the first hundred pages dealing with the breeding of domestic pigeons. Irony Number Two: the book that established the theory of evolution as the reigning interpretation of how we came to exist never actually uses the word evolution; Darwin's preferred term is "descent with modification." A third irony: although his ideas were among the most radical and controversial in history, Charles Darwin himself was an inoffensive and almost timid character, completely conventional in most of his attitudes, desirous more of solitude than celebrity.

Darwin (1809–1882) did have some freewheeling for-bears. We know that his grandfather Erasmus was a free-thinker, a close associate of the chemist and Unitarian minister Joseph Priestley and a reputable scientist in his own right. His father, Robert, was also a skeptic in religious matters, but the women of the family seem to have been more pious in their training, and Charles inherited this tension between faith and doubt. As a young man, he studied medicine but was revolted by the sight of blood. He seems to have been headed for a career as a country vicar—not because of any priestly calling, apparently, but because a parson's life back then offered the leisure to collect beetles (one of Darwin's early enthusiasms) and pursue the independent study of what in those days was called "natural philosophy." He might have taken ordination in the Church of England, until he received a better offer, to travel as captain's companion aboard the H.M.S. Beagle on its five-year voyage of discovery. And it was aboard ship, from his researches on plant and animal life and from a reading of Thomas Malthus's *An Essay on the Principle of Population*, that Darwin came to his penetrating but simple insight of how life evolved, through random variation and natural selection. In the course of reproduction, every organism typically produces more offspring than can possibly survive, and those to whom chance has given a slight advantage—a tougher hide, or a bigger brain—will tend to prevail over their competitors and reproduce in kind, passing on those favorable traits in a cumulative process that over the course of the millennia has taken us from a single-celled ancestor to the amazing multiplicity of life.

Darwin was not the first to propose that life develops and changes over time. Indeed, his own grandfather Erasmus had asked the question:

> *Would it be too bold to imagine, that in the great length of time, since the earth began to exist, perhaps millions of ages before the commencement of the history of mankind, would it be too bold to imagine, that all warm-blooded animals have arisen from one living filament which the Great First Cause endued with animality?*

What the grandson glimpsed that had escaped his predecessors was a mechanism for how this biological legerdemain took place, a mechanism that relied on purely naturalistic causes without invoking a Great First Cause or any other pseudonym for deity. *Sans* supernaturalism and without the help of revelation, Darwin had offered a compelling explanation for how life came to be.

And yet he himself resisted his own conclusions. More than twenty years lapsed between the time when

Darwin ended his trip on the Beagle and the year 1859, when he finally gathered the nerve to publish his own thoughts and conclusions, forced into print only because another investigator, Alfred Russell Wallace (1823–1913), seemed close to stealing Darwin's thunder. Why a twenty-year delay in broadcasting his findings to the wider world, twenty long years of postponement and procrastination during which Darwin occupied himself largely with a study on the sex lives of barnacles? One possible explanation is that Darwin had no desire to promulgate a theory with such incendiary implications. He was fearful of the religious firestorm he knew it might engender. He himself seemed hopelessly divided in his outlook, acknowledging in his *Autobiography* "the extreme difficulty or rather impossibility of conceiving this immense and wonderful universe, including man with his capacity for looking far backwards and far into futurity, as the result of blind chance or necessity," elsewhere calling himself an agnostic who could not believe in Christianity because he found it unsupported by the evidence. To a friend late in life, he confessed that "my theology is simply a muddle," and the muddle that Darwin created has continued to grow for many people right to the present day.

Americans, being among the most religious people in the world, are probably more muddled than most. For instance, a recent survey undertaken by George Bishop at the University of Cincinnati found that forty-four percent of all Americans subscribe to a literal reading of the creation story found in the book of Genesis. (That's right. Almost half of all people living in the United States believe we are descended from Adam and Eve.) Of practicing scientists who were polled, a majority agreed with the statement that "humans developed over millions of years from less advanced forms of life, and God had no part in this process." The conflict occasionally erupts into electoral politics. In 1999, the Kansas Board of Education voted 6 to 4 to remove the concept of evolution from the state's science curriculum, dropping any discussion of the Big Bang for good measure. A board that was voted in the following year reversed the creationist ruling and restored good sense to the prairie state. But Darwin's theory is more frequently ignored than openly defied. For instance, in a course I teach as a volunteer in our local public schools, designed to acquaint students with some of the basic principles of ecology, the word *evolution* is never mentioned in the curriculum—rather like teaching a course on chemistry without discussing atomic theory. In fact, the analogy is rather good. Both evolution and atomic theory are just that—theories—but they are the indispensable, unifying theories within their respective fields that give order and coherence to everything else, the vast array of compounds and elemental substances that make up the physical world on the one hand, the incredible diversity of creatures that inhabit our biosphere on the other. It's a scandal that seventy years after the Scopes trial evolution is still off limits in far too many classrooms.

The reason, of course, is that Darwin is seen as the enemy of religion. For some, his theory seemed to remove all trace of miracle and mystery from creation. When Darwin's theory was published, for instance, the great American landscape artist Frederic Church (1826–1900) lost much of his inspiration for painting. He had been the highest-paid and most popular artist of the day, a master of brushwork but also the descendant of six generations of Yankee preachers who imparted a deeply moral tone to his canvases. Church was known for works that celebrated the majesty and splendor of the natural world. His depiction of Niagara Falls, painted on gargantuan scale (3.5 feet by 7.5 feet), became one of his most famous landscapes, an icon of the untamed beauty of the American frontier. Other paintings, like *The Heart of the Andes*, were more than revels in the grandiosity of nature; they were also reflections on the sublimity of God's design, which reached from the misty mountain peaks of Peru down to the smallest foreground details of hummingbirds and parrots flitting through the varied foliage of a sunlit tropical forest. Ironically, *The Heart of the Andes* was first exhibited in 1859—precisely the year that saw the publication of Darwin's *magnum opus*. Partly due to declining health, but partly due to a loss of enthusiasm, Church's output declined both in quantity and quality after the 1860s. The world that had once seemed filled with meaning and beneficence felt now cold and grim. Beneath the surface beauty of creation lurked a merciless struggle for survival—nature red in tooth and claw. Since nature had lost its divine visage, Church turned to manmade relics for a glimpse of God's presence. A trip abroad took him to the Middle East—Alexandria, Beirut, Jerusalem and Petra—as though searching the Holy Land for sources of lost inspiration. But the canvases he produced were mostly of ruined antiquities, like the Parthenon, surrounded by rubble and illumined in the rays of a sinking sun. Human striving itself seemed empty, for *Homo sapiens* could no longer be seen as the crowning glory of the cosmos.

It may be the nature of scientific revolutions to shatter human arrogance. That was the opinion of Stephen Jay Gould, for instance, who began his course on the "History of Life" by reminding students how our inflated self-image has repeatedly been reduced in size, first by Copernicus, who removed our planet from the center of the universe, then by Darwin, who showed that our species was only one among many. Perhaps some people's pedestals have been lowered a notch. Yet with all admiration and respect for Professor Gould, who passed away as I was writing this book, but who gave my kids fossils and many fond memories when they visited his musty office in the old Museum of Comparative Zoology, I have to tell you that human arrogance is alive and well. Charles Darwin did little to tarnish Gould's self-image or shrink his enormous ego, which was always as big as the dinosaurs he wrote about. A tendency to self-importance may be one of the defining marks of our kind—a part of human nature that doesn't change—and it's easy to see that a touch of hubris might have definite survival value. Narcissism could well be a product of "the selfish gene."

Harder to explain is our incurable spirituality, our tendency to self-transcendence, to mysticism, a trait that even the most hard-core secularists seem to share. "Our world does contain sacred objects and places," affirmed Dr. Gould in one of his essays.

Last night, I watched the sun set over the South African savanna — the original location and habitat of our australopithecine ancestors. The air became chill; the sounds of the night began, the incessant repetition of toad and insect, laced with an occasional and startling mammalian growl; the Southern Cross appeared in the sky, with Jupiter, Mars and Saturn ranged in a line above the arms of Scorpio. I sensed the awe, fear and mystery of the night. I am tempted to say (describing emotions, not making any inferences about realities, higher or lower) that I felt close to the origin of religion as a historical phenomenon of the human psyche. I also felt kinship in that moment with our most distant human past – for an Australopithecus africanus may once have stood, nearly three million years ago, on the same spot in similar circumstances, juggling (for all I know) that same mixture of awe and fear.

Somewhere deep-rooted in the human heart or mind, there is a presentiment of unity, of connection to something larger and older than our own rather ephemeral egos, an awareness (as Gould says) of sacred times and places.

Now Gould was careful not to call this experience God, yet others are drawn to theistic language, which to me seems equally appropriate for what's being described. Of course, I'm not suggesting the kind of God who shapes Adam from the clay like a potter or creates Eve out of Adam's rib. Intelligent believers have always known that the stories of Genesis were myths and metaphors, to be taken seriously but not literally, so that even such an orthodox theologian as C.S. Lewis could write that "in Christianity God is not a static thing—not even a person—but a dynamic, pulsating activity, a life, almost a kind of drama. Almost, if you will not think me irreverent, a kind of dance."

Following Lewis' lead, one could say that each of us is a participant in the ever-changing choreography of life. For life is ultimately a dance and not a duel. The phrase "survival of the fittest," is not even Darwin's own, but was coined by Herbert Spencer, several years before *The Origin of Species* was ever written. Spencer and others capitalized on Darwin's achievement to popularize their own economic and political agenda of unbridled competition. But competition is only one of the engines of evolutionary change. Cooperation is the other, and in the end, *eros* is even stronger than *thanatos*. What better way to describe the co-adapted courtship between the Ophryus orchid—lasciviously ornamented with just the right combination of protrusions and hairs to resemble a tantalizing female—and the male insect that is drawn to the flower to pollinate it, than as an elaborate *pas de deux*? And to call that dance divine is no more far-fetched than it is to call the sunset beautiful. To say that the violet hues of twilight are lovely to the eye is not to contradict any of the laws of optics or astronomy. Everyone knows how the light is refracted through the upper atmosphere and broken in its constituent colors. We need not claim that the sun is actually sinking through the sky or deny the rotation of the earth. For when we say the sunset is beautiful, all we are saying is that our proper human response to the western horizon at the end of day is one of pleasure, appreciation and delight. There is really no need to stop painting sunsets, or singing about them or writing poems in their praise. And to say that the dance of life is divine, similarly, we need not deny any of the data of biology or paleontology. We are merely saying that there is something quite glad and solemn in these rituals of coupling between the blossom and the bee, and that the correct and healthiest response to this wondrous dance is amazement and reverence, mixed with the humble knowledge that our species is merely one small part of an intricate pattern that has brought us into being and carries us forward in its never-to-be-repeated procession.

Such reverence is sorely needed now. For the dancers in earth's cotillion are faltering in their steps and beginning to leave the floor, one by one. "The speed at which species are being lost is much faster than any we've seen in the past—including those related to meteor collisions," according to biodiversity expert Daniel Simberloff. The lush jungles that Frederic Church celebrated in paintings like *The Andes of Ecuador* (1855) and *In the Tropics* (1856) really are in danger of losing their mystique—not because of Darwinism, of course, but due to logging, mining, agribusiness and other human despoilation.

Church had been drawn to the equatorial climes precisely by their unparalleled profusion of biomes (climactic zones like deciduous forests and mountain desert that host distinctive *flora* and *fauna*). Of *Tequendama Falls, near Bogatá, New Granada* (1854), a depiction of a 670-foot high chasm of water in Colombia, Church enthused that at "the top of the fall you are in what is called the cold country with the trees and plants and fruits of temperate climates; at the bottom grow palms, oranges, etc." Such contrasts and juxtapositions not only made for spectacular landscapes; they also gave rise to a luxuriance of speciation. And Church strove not merely for painterly effects in his scenes. He also aimed at scientific accuracy in his renderings, convinced that the tropics revealed, as nowhere else on earth, the prolific and ingenious handiwork of God.

But now clear-cutting is reducing the size of the world's tropical forests by one percent annually. In the rain forests of southern Mexico, nineteen million acres have been denuded since 1993. A large majority of the world's biologists believe that a global mass extinction is already underway and that, unless immediate action is taken, up to one fifth of all living species will disappear forever within the next thirty years. Whether the evolutionary dance can survive such a catastrophic loss — or whether the rhythms that have maintained the beat of life for billions of years will simply come to an end — has become an open question.

How that question is answered depends partly on whether or not we can again learn to view the world with an artist's eye, to see the hand of divinity within all living beings. And there is no reason that science should make us blind to the sacred in its prolific expressions. God is in the details — the lavishness and extravagance that bless every niche, nook and cranny of creation, so that out of the millions of species who inhabit our globe, not one creature has been left half-painted, merely sketched in or without a role to play within the bigger picture. "There is grandeur in this view of life," wrote Charles Darwin in the final sentence to *The Origin of Species*. "From so simple a beginning endless forms most beautiful and most wonderful have been, and are being evolved." And while we will never look at ourselves in quite the same way again after coming to the end of the book, neither will the human race ever stop wondering or worshiping — even after Darwin.

A PASSIONATE
EPISTEMOLOGY

8

An undergraduate psychology classroom is not the place people usually hear voices or see visions. But that is where a nineteen-year-old sophomore at UCLA was sitting, wondering what to do with her life, when she received the revelation that would shape the rest of her future. The year was 1965. When the lecturer referred in passing to a young British woman living in Africa with chimpanzees, one of the students "heard a song from far away, a crystal-clear chime in the distance." She thought it odd at the time—the kind of thing that only happens in movies. But the bell-like summons was impossible to ignore.

At the moment the distant chime sounded,
I knew he was talking about me. I wasn't
British and I wasn't interested in chim-

panzees. But something within me stirred. I am reminded of a line by theoretical physicist Stephen Hawking . . . "If we can remember the past, why can't we remember the future?" At that precise moment, I remembered the future. I remembered the future with such clarity that the moment remains in my mind as if it were engraved on glass.

As is often the case, a scientific career had its beginning in a moment of spiritual awakening. Biruté Galdikas had never heard of Jane Goodall before then, but she knew from this "mystical incident" that she, too, was born to study apes. It was not the kind of knowledge she could have gathered from any of her textbooks. Hers was a certainty born from within.

Apparently, there are different ways of seeing the world and differing ways of experiencing reality. We can survey it from a critical distance or become more intimately involved in the knowing. We can measure, quantify and analyze; yet there remain aspects of the world that are ineffable, insights that go beyond the bounds of language. There are some things we know with the intellect and others we can only know through empathy and the sharing of a glance, or from the upwelling of subterranean springs. Stereotypically, these separate modes of knowing are associated with science and religion. Science strives for rigor, while faith aims at rapture.

Some of these differences, moreover, appear to be gender related. While it is always dangerous to generalize about the sexes, women may have perceptual gifts and abilities that most men lack. Probably these differences are culturally selected rather than innate. And variations within the sexes are just as great as any differences between them. Obviously, girls can be tough and boys can be gentle.

But to some extent, men and women in our culture are encouraged to play to differing strengths. And this would help to explain how it was that three women — Jane Goodall, Dian Fossey and Biruté Galdikas — came to change the map of modern science with their research on the lives of the Great Apes: the chimpanzee, the mountain gorilla and the orangutan. It may be because they were women that they were able to perceive features of the world that had eluded the sensibilities of male biologists. In the process, they demonstrated how the *yang* of hard science must be balanced with the *yin* of a softer touch.

The story of these three women is told in Sy Montgomery's marvelous book, *Walking with the Great Apes*. All three were protégés of the famous paleontologist Louis Leakey. Born in Kenya in 1903, Leakey was the son of English missionaries, but always considered himself first and foremost an African in outlook. Even in old age, long after having attained world renown for his discoveries of fossils establishing Africa as the birthplace of the human race, Leakey continued to think and dream in Kikuyu, the language of the tribe into which he had been initiated as a boy of thirteen. His teacher had been a man named Joshua, of mixed Kikuyu and Ndorobo blood, who taught Louis about the habits of the native creatures: mongoose, jackal, aardvark and hyena. His unusual upbringing gave him an outsider's perspective on Western science. Firsthand observation, Leakey believed, was often more important than academic training in learning about the world.

This lesson was borne out for him in one of his first discoveries when he was only twelve years old. A cousin in England sent the young boy a book describing the flint tools of stone-age men and women. Inspired, Leakey decided to look for flint tools in his own neighborhood. What he eventually found were not flint tools at all. In fact, his parents dismissed the curious rocks he showed them as pieces of broken glass. But the curator at a Nairobi museum correctly identified Louis's find as pieces of worked obsidian. They were indeed stone-age implements. Had he known what flint looked like, Leakey later observed, he never would have picked up the tools at all. Youthfulness and lack of schooling, he concluded, are no impediments to scientific advancement.

Leakey was fascinated with human origins, and he was convinced that studies of our nearest biological relatives could help shed light on the behavior and development of our early human ancestors. But many people believed that even the unconventional Louis Leakey had finally gone mad when he chose for the first long-term study of the wild chimpanzee a secretarial school dropout named Jane Goodall. She lacked a college degree, much less any training in the life sciences. Three years later, Leakey chose another improbable candidate to investigate the mountain gorilla—Dian Fossey, an occupational therapist whose failing grades in chemistry and physics at San Jose State College had barred her from her childhood ambition of becoming a veterinarian. At her interview, Fossey found herself enumerating all the reasons she was unqualified for the venture: "I had no training in anthropology, ethology, biology, zoology or any of the other 'ologies.' Leakey scoffed, 'I have no use for overtrained people. I prefer those who are not specifically educated for this field since they go into the work with open minds and without prejudice and preconceptions." Only Biruté Galdikas, the third of Leakey's "ape girls," had scholarly credentials that might possibly have prepared her to study the elusive orangutans of Borneo. But even in her case, it was not her degree in anthropology or academic promise that caught Leakey's attention. He selected each of the women for a more intuitive, feminine quality.

In part, he felt that women were simply better observers than men. It was his wife Mary, after all, who actually deserved credit for some of Leakey's most spectacular fossil finds. Then, too, he believed that women might have more patience for the kind of long-term studies he had in mind. Leakey's own digs in the Olduvai Gorge had required twenty-five years of sifting through the sands of time before finally lighting on the fragments of *Zinjanthropus* that would push the timeline of our African genesis back two million years. The field studies he contemplated would require a similar persistence. To truly learn about the lives of apes, Leakey was sure that the animals would have to be observed over decades, from birth through maturity and old age. But in the publish-or-perish world of the university, most researchers wanted quick data and overnight breakthroughs. Women, Leakey felt, were given to a longer perspective than men. The maternal tasks of rearing children and nurturing a family cultivated skills and attitudes that do not necessarily expect an immediate reward or quick payoff. On a more practical level, Leakey also reasoned that women would be less likely than men to excite aggressive tendencies in other male primates.

Whether right or wrong, Leakey's hunch paid off. The twenty-six year old Englishwoman who stepped into the forests of the Gombe Stream Reserve to study chimpanzees would become one of the most widely recognized scientists in the world. Jane Goodall became the first to discover that chimpanzees not only use tools but make them as well, that they organize to hunt cooperatively, much in the fashion of our early human progenitors, and that their intelligence is much more closely akin to our own than had ever been imagined. Her work and that of her two colleagues profoundly changed the way we understand the human place in nature.

In the popular understanding of the time, chimpanzees were pictured as wild and violent creatures and gorillas as fierce and dangerous beasts of the jungle. But the work of Jane Goodall and Dian Fossey destroyed such stereotypes forever. They showed us the gentle side of the Great Apes: their long and playful childhood so similar to our own, their warm hugs and great openmouthed kisses of greeting and affection. "Gestures that we see performed by captive apes, such as kissing, hugging and hand-holding, are not learned imitations of humans, but common forms of expression that we humans share with the great apes," Galdikas comments.

"Apparently, kissing has a long evolutionary history." Goodall was eventually forced to revise her initial estimates of the chimps as easy-going pacifists and amiable clowns. Later findings showed that chimpanzees, like their human cousins, conduct something very like organized warfare; even more disturbing, some individuals engage in kidnapping and cannibalizing the infants of other chimps. When Jane Goodall received the first reports from her research assistants that Pom and Passion, a mother and her daughter, had stolen and eaten the child of Melissa, another member of the troop, she was incredulous that the animals she referred to in her first book as *My Friends the Wild Chimpanzees* were capable of such ruthless acts. Yet the truth is that these complex creatures seem to mirror both the best and worst aspects of human nature, with a capacity for both cooperation and aggression.

That is partly because chimpanzees are culture-bearing creatures, just like us. Adam Clark Arcadi, an anthropologist from Cornell University working in the Kibale National Park in Uganda, recently found male chimps there thumping with their palms on the huge roots of trees, producing satisfying bass-register *ka-booms* with their hand-drumming. Each animal created individualized rhythms that could last anywhere from a few seconds to half a minute and be heard up to a mile away.

Chimps at the nearby Tai National Park also drum, but sing along with pant-hoots as well, suggesting that their musicality is not innate, but varies according to each troop's local traditions.

Tool use is also culturally transmitted. One band of chimpanzees in West Africa routinely swings heavy stones to crack the nutritious panda nuts that form a big part of their diet. Calibrating the force required is difficult. Up to a ton of pressure may be needed to split the outer husk, but if pounded too hard the nut shatters and becomes inedible. Chimps have been observed carefully collecting proper pounding stones, flat on one side yet easy to grasp on the other, sometimes passing on particularly well-suited stones to the next generation. The technique has been taught and transferred from elders to youngsters for many years, yet other chimps in nearby regions have not yet learned this useful skill.

And while the *Pan troglodytes* were not as peaceable as Goodall first believed, other members of the chimpanzee family do seem to have stepped right out of Eden. Bonobos or "pygmy chimps" live within the Congo Basin and belong to the genus *Pan paniscus*. The bonobos resolve most of their conflicts and relieve social tension through sex play, rather than through violence or aggression. So saying what constitutes "natural" chimpanzee behavior is as difficult as defining what's normal for *Homo sapiens*. Some subcultures may be far more bellicose than others.

Perhaps the chimps that Dr. Goodall first observed were simply won over by her friendly approach. Most animals — including people — respond positively to loving-kindness and when treated with good manners will respond in kind. The "ferocity" of many creatures may be more a function of our own fear and projected hostility than of any intrinsic savagery. And so the chimps Goodall observed may have been on their best behavior, at least in the beginning. In biology, as in physics, the perceiver partly determines the nature of what is perceived. In our own species, for example, research has shown repeatedly that children labeled as smart will outperform their peers; those stigmatized as troublemakers usually descend to the level of lowered expectation. Dr. Goodall was prepared to see what was best in her subjects, and the chimps happily obliged.

Women appear to bring a different angle of vision to their interactions than most men. A study by the psychologists Susan Pollak and Carol Gilligan explores this gender variation. They showed sample groups of men and women a picture of acrobats working together on the high wire and trapeze and then asked the two groups to write stories about the scene. They found that men were significantly more likely to write tales involving violence and betrayal. In one account, for instance, a man imagined a plot in which one acrobat purposely drops his partner, who plunges to her death below. Women, on the other hand, were more likely to construct stories in which teamwork and trust are the prevailing motifs. Many women imagined the presence of a "safety net" protecting the performers from mishap, even though the actual picture contained no such net. Women were more inclined than men to perceive the world as a caring and nurturing environment.

Caring was a quality each of the women brought to her scientific investigation. Galdikas, Fossey and Goodall were anything but detached clinicians. The prevailing orthodoxy of the time declared that researchers should not be emotionally involved with the animals they studied. Such bonding, it was thought, might interfere with scientific "objectivity." But Jane Goodall broke this rule early on. Wise old Flo, the dignified David Graybeard and the other chimps she studied were for her individuals, full of personality that demanded an emotional response. Even so, the first paper Jane submitted for scientific publication was rejected by the editor. He insisted she number the chimps instead of naming them. Wherever Jane had written "he" or "she" to identify an individual animal, the editor had crossed out the personal pronoun with a red pencil and substituted "it." Yet ultimately, it was Jane Goodall's empathy, her sense of compassion, her intuitive feeling of kinship with her animal companions that enabled her to see so keenly into their lives and habits. As she wrote in *The Chimpanzees of Gombe*, "I readily admit to a high level of emotional involvement with individual chimpanzees—without which, I suspect, the research would have come to an end many years ago."

Together, the women introduced an entirely new approach in the biological sciences. Until then, most of the study of primate behavior had taken place in the antiseptic confines of the laboratory. Animals were manipulated in experiments that tested their reaction to artificial stimuli. One of the most famous researchers of the 1950s and 60s, for instance, was Harry Harlow (1905–1981), whose work on maternal deprivation is still cited in many high school and college textbooks. Separating infant monkeys from their mothers at birth, Harlow provided them with "surrogate mothers" made of wire mesh and terry cloth. The babies hugged the soft objects, seeking warmth and protection. Then, at the touch of the experimenter's button, metal spikes sprang out from the mother's body, jabbing the unsuspecting infant. Another wire-mesh mother hit the helpless baby with a high-pressure blast of air ("It would blow the animal's skin practically off its body," according to Harlow), and yet another surrogate was devised which could be rapidly lowered in temperature, from 99° to 35° Fahrenheit, giving the "cold shoulder" to the rejected youngster. Other infants were placed into stainless steel cylinders, deprived of cuddling and ordinary sensory contact, until they finally went psychotic. Harlow thereby "proved" that mental illness results from poor mothering.

In contrast to a scientific method that confined animals and subjected them to electric shocks or other inhumane treatment, Goodall, Fossey and Galdikas each studied their subjects in the wild. They sought to engage the animals in their own world and on their own terms. Their relationship to the apes did not rest on dominating them or controlling them. Rather, each waited patiently, sometimes for months, for the animals to invite them to share their world. Of course, chimps and gorillas can quickly outpace a human in the forests. The swamps where orangutans make their arboreal home are easily passable for those who live in treetops, but nearly impenetrable at ground level. There is literally no way to study these creatures up close without their full consent. So each of the women had to announce her peaceful intentions, like Dian Fossey, mimicking the gorillas' facial mannerisms as she gradually drew near, munching wild celery stalks and belching contentment grunts (a husky throated *naooom*) on the rain-drenched mountains

of Rwanda until the neighboring gorillas finally understood that she meant no harm and one would come forth
to gingerly touch her hand. Eventually, Dian would be
able to get close to animals emotionally as well as physi-
cally. Her favorite, Digit, would frequently invite her to
play, tumbling to his back with stumpy legs waving in
the air as if to say "How can you resist me?" At such
moments, says Fossey, she felt her scientific "detach-
ment" dissolve. On another occasion, she wrote:

> I heard a noise in the foliage by my side and looked
> directly into the beautifully trusting face of Macho,
> who stood gazing up at me. She had left her group to
> come to me. On perceiving the softness, the tranquilli-
> ty, and trust conveyed by Macho's eyes, I was over-
> whelmed by the extraordinary depth of our rapport.
> The poignancy of her gift will never diminish.

These were scientists who sought knowledge, not by
achieving mastery over nature, but by becoming fully
sensitive and receptive to the natural world. It was a
knowing that engaged the heart as well as the mind.

The way we know — how we undergird our beliefs
and muster the authority to make them credible — is
called "epistemology." The term is related to *pistis*, a
Greek word that can mean both "faith" and "knowl-

edge." Religion and science alike are concerned with how we access the truth and gain insight into reality. In many ways this is the primary question for every field of inquiry. Shall we rely on abstract reasoning or gut feelings? Trust solely in the testimony of senses or listen also to the promptings of the still small voice within? There is little we can discuss, in fact, without first asking how we know what we know.

And there are epistemological lessons for us in the work of Jane Goodall, Dian Fossey and Biruté Galdikas. One lesson is that each of us has access to the truth. At the beginning of Jane Goodall's career, many experts and authorities were skeptical of her abilities. They were doubtful due to her lack of professional training, and many were scornful because of her sex. Other scientists made frequent references to the "blonde bimbo," recalls her editor at *National Geographic*, and were derisive because her methodologies were unconventional and untried. When Jane Goodall discovered that chimpanzees use wands of grass to fish for termites, some scientists whispered that she must have taught the animals to make these tools. How could something so fundamental have been overlooked by other researchers? ("You have to obtain a union card in the scientific field," Fossey complained. "Without a Ph.D. at the least, it is very hard to get adequate grant support or to get really good students to come and work on your project. Without that Big Degree, you don't cut much ice no matter how good you are.") These women demonstrated once again that wisdom and understanding are not the monopoly of any special priesthood—clerical or scientific—still less the exclusive property of a single sex, but are freely available to all who honestly inquire at their gates.

Moral issues, in particular, are too important to be left to the discretion of any band of experts. Researchers frequently have hidden agendas or may have ethical blind spots of which they themselves are not even aware, and the work of these three women alerts us to be on guard against any methodology that purports to be "value-free." Assigning numbers rather than names to laboratory animals, for example, may appear as an "objective" approach to science when it is actually *objectifying:* transforming living creatures with individual preferences and personalities into mere biological units. Controlling the variables in an experiment is essential to scientific investigation, but can also mask an unhealthy obsession with controlling life itself (as with Harry Harlow, who proposed varying the size and shape of his isolation chambers to observe the effect on infant primates). Dr. William Lemmon, Director of the Institute for Primate Studies at the University of Oklahoma in the 1950s and '60s, was another psychologist obsessed with maternal deprivation studies. Lemmon kept "discipline" over his chimps with two-by-fours, cattle prods and pellet guns. According to Roger Fouts, who was on the OU faculty at the time, his methods were so effective that the chimpanzees would approach him in a submission posture, crouching low to the ground with one wrist extended limply, lips pulled back in a mask of fear. Lemmon would then place his hand against the chimps' cages and have the animals kiss his ring—a coiled snake with two red rubies for eyes. One hopes that individuals like Harlow and Lemmon are the exception rather than the rule in animal labs. People who do this kind of research are probably no more prone to bullying or cruelty than the average run of humanity. But there may be something in the dynamic of the captive/captor relationship that necessarily lends itself to abuse.

Power can be bewitching, and psychologists and biologists succumb as easily as any others to the temptation to play God—especially when technology bestows seemingly superhuman abilities to create and manipulate life. Those who claim their work is above the moral fray need to recognize the extent to which arrogance and egoism contaminate almost every human undertaking, science included. Rather than striving for the unobtainable goal of being "value-free," perhaps scientists should consciously embrace a value system that honors all life and respects the feelings of others—especially those in our custody and care. Today, that would include not only the millions of creatures used in laboratory research, but also a multitude of species endangered or at risk, whose survival is wrapped up with our own.

The work of Jane Goodall, Dian Fossey and Biruté Galdikas shows that sympathy and compassion are not obstacles to understanding the world, but may be the bridges that carry us to greater insight. Indeed, it may be necessary to be enamored with the world in order to fully know the world. *Pistis* (knowledge) needs to be linked to *philia* (love). A science that claims to be dispassionate, unfeeling toward the life it studies, is not only callous and inhumane. Ultimately, it is poor science. "Emotional intelligence" is required along with cognitive capacity. For it is not through dominion over other living things but through a shared communion with them that we reach the most complete understanding of what it means to be alive.

These are passionate women. Jane Goodall today lectures and lobbies ceaselessly on behalf of chimpanzees whose existence in the wild is now threatened, and of other animals who are subjected to unnecessary cruelty in the laboratory. Dian Fossey died defending the harmless giants she loved against human poachers who killed them to turn their heads into trophies and their hands into ashtrays. Biruté Galdikas negotiates the intricate world of Indonesian politics in her efforts to preserve the vanishing rain forests that are home to the solitary orangutan. "I have always felt strongly that saving orangutans is as important as studying them," she declares. Each of these women has shown that not only kindness but commitment and a concern for all living beings must be united with the quest for scientific knowledge.

Knowledge can then be transmuted into wisdom—a sagacity that goes beyond the *how* of science to embrace the *why and wherefore* of faith. And wisdom, in our Western religious tradition, has always been associated with the feminine: with receptivity, with gentleness, with nurturance and the kind of interpersonal knowing that, more than any amount of formal data, allows us to experience the beating of the heart we have in common. We must love our way to a deeper knowledge of life. Tenderness and truth walk hand in hand. As Jane Goodall reminds us, "Only if we can understand can we care." But the obverse also holds. Only if we are able to care shall we fully understand.

GOD IS A VERB

In his autobiography, *The Darkness and the Light*, the philosopher Charles Hartshorne relates an early religious experience that took place when he was a soldier, stationed in France during the First World War. There was a small ledge, located a few feet under the edge of the great chalk cliffs that faced the English channel, where his regiment was garrisoned, and on that stony ledge the young man liked to sit and think, not daydreaming about wine or women or battle or any of the other preoccupations of military men, but reading William James's *The Varieties of Religious Experience* and thinking about the nature of ultimate reality. Perhaps James, who once defined "religion" as "what one does with one's solitude," was right in this particular instance, for it was in this isolated spot, with only the wheeling gulls for company, that

9

the future theologian had two pivotal experiences that would shape all his later career.

"I had been thinking of certain aspects of my life that seemed discouraging," remembers Hartshorne. "These somewhat gloomy reflections were interrupted by a simultaneous multitude of shrill sounds." Looking to his left almost vertically down to the bottom of the cliff, he saw a school playground filled with shouting, laughing French children. The contrast was enlightening. "Suppose my own life is unsatisfactory," he thought. "So what? I am a tiny fragment of human life. The rest of it is not all unfortunate or wretched. Nothing compels me to think of myself miserable rather than others—those children—happy.' Never since then," wrote Hartshorne, "have I allowed myself to identify, unless briefly, the question, Is life good and beautiful? with the question, Is my life now good and beautiful? And I have not wavered in the two convictions that there is some minimal good, beauty in all life, including my own, and that what finally matters, even to me, is the life of the Whole, the Something that includes me, outlasts me (save as I contribute myself to it), and contains more good than I can distinctly imagine."

Hartshorne's other religious experience occurred as he was looking across and up the valley, at the wide, scenic landscape. He says he had been thinking about the question of mind and matter and pondering the dualistic hypothesis that these are two irreducible kinds of reality: an outer world, governed by blind and unthinking forces, and an inner world of thought and emotion. But the rolling terrain, its vibrant greens and earth tones, its serenity and calm, convinced him otherwise. He realized, he says, that the landscape he beheld was itself endowed with feelings, was sensitive, as restless and filled with nameless stirrings as he himself. Though he did not analyze it further at the time, that instant of sympathetic identification with the world made an impression that would last.

I don't think Hartshorne is unique in his religious intuitions. Many of us have had similar experiences of feeling connected to a larger something: being drawn so deeply into the peace of a landscape that we seem to be at one with the textures and sensations of the world round about, feeling our own small and obscure destiny linked to some greater and more radiant purpose. Even brief glimpses of this kind can illuminate the rest of life. Though their intensity fades, their memory abides. Few of us, though, will go on to fully analyze such experiences, to write books about them or integrate them into an original system of philosophy.

But Charles Hartshorne, whose lifetime spanned the twentieth century (1897-2000), was one of those inventive minds not content to leave such experiences unexamined or pigeonhole them into pre-existing religious categories. The son of an Episcopal clergyman, Hartshorne abandoned his childhood beliefs after reading Emerson as an adolescent. But he would never abandon his quest to find a God who was intellectually tenable and in tune with the modern world, and in that venture he would eventually become one of the primary architects of the small but important movement known as process theology. As a technical philosopher who studied under Alfred North Whitehead (1861–1947) at Harvard and then taught at Emory and the University of Texas, his scholarly writings were never aimed at a popular audience. Yet I think it worth the effort to become better acquainted. John Cobb, Jr., who counts himself as a disciple, observes that "both directly and through his theological followers, Hartshorne has influenced the general course of theology since World War II," and though the process school has never constituted the mainstream, it has provided one of the more original voices in recent religious discourse. With an entire volume of the *Library of Living Philosophers* dedicated to his thought, Hartshorne stands in the same company as figures like Albert Einstein. And if there is any school of reflection in which I would place myself, it is here, in the circle of process thought. Perhaps, though, it is easiest to introduce his work in terms of an analogy.

As an amateur artist, who finds standing out-of-doors with brush and canvas to be one of the most satisfying and frustrating occupations imaginable, I can easily relate to Hartshorne's vision atop his lonely perch, when he looked out across the landscape of France and sensed the colors he saw — the trees, the land, the clouds, the sky — were charged with feeling, sentient almost, insistently alive. That feeling is why I paint, or try to. It explains why a decent painting can be more effective at conveying the mood and flavor and spirit of a subject than any photograph, for although the camera is an accurate recorder of light and shadow, as a mechanical device it lacks any sense of empathy. Sometimes I carry a camera to capture scenes that touch me in some manner, perhaps a tree-lined street that fills me with a sense of tranquility or quiet or domesticity, but often the snapshots I take are disappointing, lifeless and flat compared to the picture that's vivid in my memory. The emotion is missing. Sometimes I can still use even a poor photograph to re-create the scene and out of my own imagination supply some of the vitality that's lacking. Art reminds us that the world is responsive and alive, filled with both joy and pathos, and this is also one of the primary assertions of process theology. At some level, everything is capable of feeling.

And not only that; everything is connected. I suppose one of the childlike mistakes most of us make when first learning how to draw is to delineate each of our creations with a firm, dark outline. As children, we probably used a black crayon. A person, a dog, a house were all depicted with a heavy, dark border framing their edges. But in the real world there are no distinct boundaries of this kind. One of my mother's instructors in art school used to smear his thumb across her work whenever he saw an edge forming, softening and blending the contours. In a fine portrait, of course, there is no hard line where the mouth or the nose meets the rest of the face, nor in a landscape is there any disjunction that separates the mountain from the sky. There is a seamless quality to our experience. This is another of the fundamental points of process metaphysics.

And within reality, as within a work of art, all of the parts stand in mutual relation to one another. In painting, I've become more and more aware of this fact as I've tried to control my colors. Each hue and tint has an impact upon all the others, and to make them work in harmony can be a difficult undertaking. The most accomplished colorists of modern painting were undoubtedly the Impressionists, and the one who carried his investigations in this field the farthest was Georges Seurat, the father of the artistic style known as Pointillism. Probably most readers have seen his canvases, which are constructed of thousands of tiny dots, or points of color. This approach was based on Seurat's study on the physiology of perception. He was especially influenced by a text titled *The Law of Simultaneous Color Contrast,* written by Michel Eugene Chevreul in 1839. Chevreul showed that a spot of pure color on the retina is always accompanied by its complement; the eye sees a dot of orange rimmed by a halo of blue, for instance. Red is ringed by green, purple by yellow. The interference of these visual haloes means that each color affects its neighbor. None exists in isolation; they literally interpenetrate. Color perception is therefore a complex process of interaction, and what Seurat tried to demonstrate in his painting was how each point of color interrelates with those that surround it, each reciprocally impacting all the others. Seurat's finished paintings strike many observers as being rather stiff and immobile. But if we could imagine them instead in motion, like a movie or like the world itself, the waves lapping on the beach, the picnickers promenading gaily through the park, each corpuscle of light constantly changing hue in relation to all its companions, then we should have a very good analogy to the model of the universe posited by process thought, except for the detail that the units which compose our world are not made of pigment, but of events.

Process philosophy holds that materialism is mistaken. What constitutes our universe is not an assortment of lifeless particles but an ensemble of interrelated and dynamic happenings. And each of these events—from the energy that maintains a simple chemical bond to the complex flow of information through a termite mound or coral reef—is in constant change and interaction with all the others.

Try to pick out one piece of the universe to study in isolation, and you discover that it's connected to everything else. A chimpanzee, for example, cannot be understood by separating the infant from its mother to see "what happens." Every organism exists within a network of relationships—relationships between parent and offspring, predator and prey, population and food supply—that enable it to live and which it in turn touches and transforms. Even on a much simpler physical level, the same principle holds. A cloudy day may be associated with high humidity and low barometric pressure. But there are no purely linear relationships involved. A storm front doesn't cause clouds to form any more than clouds cause the storm. Weather is messier and more reciprocal than that, with a built-in unpredictability that makes long-term forecasting not just difficult but impossible. From what we know of chaos theory, a Monarch butterfly fluttering its wings in Mexico can affect siroccos in the Mediterranean, thousands of miles away. These are co-creative events.

I am an event. You are an event. So is a bear, a rain forest and the winding of the helix within us all. All are active participants within the bigger picture, the same picture Charles Hartshorne glimpsed as he looked down from his lonely heights at the carefree play of schoolchildren in France and felt his own problems grow less burdensome. Hartshorne would call that big picture God, a reality that includes all of us but is larger than any of us.

Painting with broad strokes and upon the largest canvas available, this is how we might depict the contours of the world, as seen through the lens of process thought:

- *Reality in all its manifestations is subjective as well as objective. There is a psychic or experiential dimension to all situations. We have seen how modern science confirms this. Consciousness appears to be finely interwoven into the fabric of creation, both at the relativistic level of the very large and in the quantum realm of the very small. The same mind that impels us to ask how the world fits together seems to have been at work within the universe itself, offering intelligible answers.*

- *At some incipient level, everything is alive. Atmospheres, oceans and continents, for example, are all vital organs within the larger body of Gaia. The cosmos itself, it appears, is predisposed toward the conditions that permit life to arise and flourish. Process philosophy is sometimes called "the philosophy of organism" for this reason. Not all life rises to the level of reflective awareness, but all is endowed with some capacity for creative self-expression.*

• *The whole defines its parts. As Whitehead remarks, "The misconception which has haunted philosophic literature throughout the centuries is the notion of independent existence. There is no such mode of existence. Every entity is only to be understood in terms of the way in which it is interwoven with the rest of the universe." Human beings are not distinct from nature in such a world. As star dust, we have grown out of this cosmos and are inseparable from all that is.*

• *Relationships form the matrix for our mutual becoming. Lives intermesh, thoughts and feelings intermingle. Events influence one another, not like billiard balls that collide and expend their energy in exchanges that are purely external. Rather, the relationships we share are like the bits of color in a painting, each of us a point of light, our own coloration affected by all the surrounding hues.*

Thinking of the world as composed of verbs rather than nouns — of evanescent "events" rather than enduring "substances" — involves a conceptual shift. At least since the time of Isaac Newton, we have been accustomed to imagining that what he called "solid, massy, hard, impenetrable, moveable Particles" constitute the irreducible units of our universe. Up until that time, the world was still half-enchanted, filled with "sympathies" and vague affinities that made "natural philosophy" an enterprise that was as much religious as scientific. But Newton theorized that matter is dumb and insensate partly to emphasize the glory of God, the immaterial maker and prime mover of all. He repudiated the suggestion that objects might contain any animating or "occult" qualities, the better to illustrate the need for "a powerful, ever-living Agent" to set the world in gear. Even gravity, he asserted, must owe its operations "to some other Cause than dense Matter." But physicists today are saying that reality at the most fundamental levels is composed of shimmering waves of probability, fluctuating eruptions in the void, an intertwined continuum of matter and energy that exerts invisible fields of force stretching from here to the farthest star. Neither Newton's theology nor his physics make complete sense anymore, but the idea that our world might be composed of events or "occasions of experience" (Whitehead's term) has become increasingly plausible.

Whitehead proposed that each of these "occasions" gathers and synthesizes information from its own immediate past and from its surroundings, then responds. This response—whether attraction or repulsion, affection or its opposite—is a bit of small-scale, localized world-making activity. And this response is not forced or causally overdetermined. Rather, each occasion—consciously or with dim apprehension—decides how to take account of the world it experiences round about. And its response then concretizes what had previously hovered as a mere penumbra of possibility into a manifestation of actual existence—becoming in turn part of the total environment with which other events, and its own successors, will have to contend. The "choices" a quark has may be limited, and so the universe displays a dependable, statistical regularity. Nonetheless, there is an element of subjectivity and intention in all of these events and in their interplay. And from the multitude of events taking place each moment, vanishing and giving birth to new occasions, the world in all its freshness and changeability arises.

In the classes I lead with my own congregation, I sometimes liken the process model of reality to a stimulating conversation. A conversation arises and flows without any prior plan, but with an order born of free association. As participants and learners gathered in a circle, each member of the class is an "event" — a life story in progress — who both contributes and receives. Most of us have settled opinions or fixed ideas on the topic of theology, the result of our religious upbringing and past reflection, and each wants to share his or her own views. But through listening, each may find those views changing. In many respects the conversation is predictable. Most of what can be said about God has already been mentioned over the centuries. (Bertrand Russell's remark that "there is nothing so absurd that it has not been uttered at one time or another by some philosopher" applies to theologians as well.) But the shape of the dialogue is not predetermined, despite that, and novel insights are always ready to emerge as a result of our encounter; the group can generate ideas that go beyond the additive knowledge of the individuals in the room. When the conversation ends and the class is over, few of us are likely to have been profoundly affected. But perhaps we have been altered in subtle ways — ways that we will carry over into future discussions. Our personal narrative will have been recast. When the poet Muriel Rukeyser said that "the universe is made of stories, not of atoms," she was closer to the truth than she realized. For at bottom, the world consists of a multiplicity of stories, transient creative episodes that overlap, merge or clash, yet each one striving for greater clarity of self-expression and more thorough comprehension of the whole.

This is one way to think of God: as that Living Whole of which you and I and others in the "cosmic conversation" are active parts and partners. In a mechanistic universe, such a proposition would be ridiculous, as in the cartoon where a white-coated lab technician feeds an old-fashioned, room-sized computer a punch card encoded with the question, *"Is there a God?"* After spinning its wheels and flashing its lights, the machine eventually prints out the answer: *"Now there is!"* Whatever we mean by the word God, we do not mean a machine. And when the universe was envisioned as machine-like, as for Newton, the only way to imagine deity was as a Being external and superior to all created forms. In Newton's words:

> *This Being governs all things, not as the soul of the world, but as Lord over all; and on account of his dominion he is wont to be called Lord God or Universal Ruler.*

Newton's faith stressed divine transcendence rather than immanence. He wanted no confusion between the Watchmaker and the watch. But with the demise of the clockwork universe, this theological difficulty disap-

pears, along with many of the scientific objections to theism. For there is nothing supernatural about the God
proposed by process thought, nothing otherworldly. God
is in the cosmos, though not completely identified with
the cosmos, surpassing it as the Whole exceeds the parts.
In a panoply of events, God is simply the Main Event.
Amid a multitude of partial and imperfect relationships,
God is the one to whom all are fully and perfectly related. In a "participatory universe" where all have a role in
the construction of reality, God is the one who partici-
pates in all life and every act of creation.

I like this way of thinking about God for several reasons, first of all because it is ecological. Too much of our
Western religious tradition has been human-centered.
Men and women are conceived in the divine image and
given dominion over the earth. Only human beings pos-
sess an immortal soul, and only they count in the moral
calculus. For process thinkers, in contrast, all creatures
are valued participants within the great living system. Of
course, not every entity within our world is "alive" in
any strict sense. A rock or rubble pile probably lacks the
level of internal integration to achieve even a low grade
of experience. But animals, especially, are like us in
knowing both pleasure and pain, and none is so small as
to be beneath our consideration. It's significant that
Hartshorne is almost better known as an ornithologist

than as a philosopher. As the author of *Born to Sing: A Survey of World Bird Song*, he suggests that animals, like ourselves, appreciate beauty and are endowed with an aesthetic impulse. In a celebratory universe, there are many species that savor the sheer exuberance of living—who sing for the joy of singing. And there is a divine element within every living being that shares in the chorus of life.

I like the process conception of God, too, because it makes room for freedom. In much of the Biblical tradition, God is likened to a Middle Eastern potentate: King of kings, Lord of lords. God's word is law; he speaks, and his will is done. The culture that revered this kind of deity was patriarchal from top to bottom, as well as rigidly controlled. The only genuine choices permitted were obedience and sin, and theologies that stressed divine omnipotence often had a fatalistic aspect. As in the dogma of predestination, everything that happened in the world had been foreseen from the beginning of time, divinely foreordained. But in process thought, we do have alternatives. Our options are very real. There is no finished blueprint that determines the historical process or guarantees its outcome. For as we realize now, we live in an open-ended cosmos. Not only the future, but perhaps even the past (scientists tell us) is still partially undetermined. Some events are unpredictable, not only because of the chaos inherent in such seemingly simple actions as the flip of a coin, but because spontaneity and originality are inevitably part of the equation within any universe that includes beings like ourselves. For better or worse, we make our own destiny, and through a multitude of decisions large and small we shape the course of our own evolution. God is involved in that process, not as a commanding or coercive presence, but as a persuasive lure, the promise of richer, more rewarding experiences to those who choose wisely and well.

The same deity that was considered to be an all powerful overseer was also thought to be "immutable," meaning incapable of suffering or feeling injury. Sensitivity was synonymous with weakness (it meant you could get hurt). In process theology, by contrast, God's perfection is the gift of absolute empathy and rapport. God is the One who rejoices in each creature's ecstasy and also feels their anguish—for God is as closely related to each of us as the Whole is related to its parts. Of course, this image of deity is also present in the Bible, in tension with that of the patriarchal monarch. God is love, the ever-present possibility of intimacy and compassion. The kind of influence this divinity exercises is not *power-over* but *power-with*: nurturing and deepening the bonds of kinship that hold us in human community and keep us in right relation with other living beings. For the downtrodden or downhearted, God's power lies in the seductive suggestion that a freer, more fulfilling existence is possible. In a world we often experience as discordant, in conflict, at cross-purposes with itself, God is the real potential for healing and unity present in each moment.

Finally, I like process thought because it offers hope to the human spirit and encourages us to take responsibility for our lives—for as each of us shapes the world, we also add to the life of God. C.S. Lewis's image of God as the evolutionary "dance" in which we live and move seems an apt expression here. Or, to return to our original formulation, we might think of God as the Big Picture, the ongoing creative endeavor that includes us all and to whom each of us contributes a minor brush stroke or two. It is comforting to believe that our little lifetimes add to the larger composition in some small way. Even the layers of experience that have slipped into the past—the underpainting—continue to influence the work-in-progress, and as artists realize, the most minute highlights can often have a telling effect upon the total canvas. Indeed, if the Butterfly Effect is valid, our words and actions may have a larger and more far-reaching impact than most of us dare to believe. And although our time here is, as Whitehead said, a "perpetual perishing," nothing that we have ever said or done is entirely wasted or discarded, but serves to feed and nourish the world in its endless process of becoming.

Religion, according to Alfred North Whitehead, is a phenomenon that begins in wonder and ends in wonder. Feelings of awe, reverence and gratitude are primary, and these can never be learned from books. We gain them from sitting high on a cliff side, gazing at the sea, lost in reverie and listening to the laughter of children. But I appreciate those individuals like Whitehead and Charles Hartshorne who muse deeply about such experiences and what they mean.

Their intellectual edifice is admittedly metaphysical rather than physical — not an effort to do science, but an attempt to think about reality at the highest levels of generality and abstraction. Yet because Whitehead was one of the outstanding mathematicians of the twentieth century and quite familiar with the new physics, his philosophy is entirely consistent with the universe of relativity and quantum theory. As a mental map, process thought is not intended to describe every detail of our world, but to indicate the grand outlines of our experience, including religious experience.

And here is the testimony of my own religious experience: "*A human being is a part of the whole called by us universe, a part limited in time and space.*" These words of Einstein, with which I prefaced this book, have become a touchstone for me. They speak to the spiritual intuition that we are related in mind and body to an all-encompassing reality, a reality that is unimaginably old and yet somehow always new. In at-one-ment and alignment with this reality, our own well-being resides. *"We experience ourselves, our thoughts and feelings as something separated from the rest, a kind of optical delusion of consciousness. This delusion is a kind of prison for us, restricting us to our personal desires and to affection for a few persons nearest to us."* Yet we are an outgrowth of the same process that produced the universe in all its splendor, and our own identity is inseparable from the relational synergy that vivifies our cosmos. *"Our task must be to free ourselves from this prison by widening our circle of compassion to embrace all living creatures and the whole of nature in its beauty."* It may no longer be possible to believe in a deity that is omnipotent or immutable, but in the One who accompanies all creation and invites us to expand the horizons of our concern to all the earth, we can still affirm that God is Life and God is Love. It may no longer be appropriate to pray to a Lord who is ruler of the universe, standing outside of nature, intervening from above. But with the Living Whole as our companion, then even in our moments of inwardness and solitude, we can never really be abandoned or alone.

ELEPHANTS ALL
THE WAY DOWN

10

A story is told of William James, the great psychologist and author of *The Varieties of Religious Experience*. In his travels, James encountered an Indian holy man from whom he hoped to learn more of the Hindu religion. James had read the creation myth of the Hindus, in which Brahma, the creator, brings the world into being and then places it upon the backs of four celestial elephants to support its corners. And so he inquired about the myth: "I understand that you believe the world rests upon the backs of four white elephants. Is that correct?" "Indeed, this is so," replied the holy man. "Good," James went on. "Now tell me, just what is it that stands beneath the great white elephants?" "In each case," the sage replied, "there stands another great white elephant." "And what is beneath that set of elephants?" James pressed on. "Why, four more elephants." "But tell me what stands under all of the elephants," James insisted. "Dr. James, Dr. James," the Hindu replied patiently, "don't you understand? It's great white elephants, all the way down!"

In his book *The Mask of Religion*, Peter Fleck remembers hearing a similar myth as a boy in grade school. "It described the vision of the universe held by a Hindu tribe somewhere in India," Fleck recalls. "Its members believed that the earth and the sky above it rest on an elephant and that the elephant stands on a turtle."

> *I remember that I was troubled by one particular aspect of the story. It was not the role of the elephant. Maybe I had already heard of Atlas, to whom the Greeks imparted a similar role; if so, the analogy may have reassured me. Nor did I feel disturbed by the idea of this obviously mythical elephant resting on an equally mythical turtle. What did bother me was that nobody apparently had raised the question: And what does the turtle rest on? It was the absence of that question, let alone a satisfactory answer to it, that made me feel, as a young boy, that our Western way of thinking was superior to what I experienced to be the primitive ways of the East.*

As he matured, Fleck says, he came to appreciate the wisdom contained in the story. For every discovery seems to raise new questions. The latest findings in science are superseded by later findings. And just when you seem to be getting to the bottom of things, the foundation begins to drop out. Everything appears to rest on a turtle, who in turn rests on nothing.

The universe is ultimately a mystery. As it says in the book of Job, "God stretches out the north over the void, and hangs the world upon nothing." Why does anything exist? Why this particular universe of carbon-based life forms and daytime soap operas instead of some possibly more rational world? These questions may seem far removed from daily living, but trying for even a moment to imagine nothing instead of something — no space, no duration, no observer, nothing to observe — brings on a sensation close to vertigo, like having the ground drop away beneath one's feet.

"One need only shut oneself in a closet," says William James — and it is easy to imagine James, the pragmatist, carrying out this experiment himself — "and begin to think of the fact of one's being there, of one's queer bodily shape in the darkness . . . of one's fantastic character and all, to have the wonder steal over the detail as much as over the general fact of being, and to see that it is only familiarity that blunts it. Not only that anything should be, but that this very thing should be, is mysterious! Philosophy stares, but brings no reasoned solution, for from nothing to being there is no logical bridge."

"To that strange, disquieting question, *'Why does anything exist?'* science can never hope to provide an answer," agrees Martin Gardner. "Why does the apple fall? Because of the law of gravitation? Why the law of gravitation? Because of certain equations that are part of the theory of relativity. Should physicists succeed some day in writing one ultimate equation from which all physical laws can be derived, one could still ask, 'Why that equation?' If physicists reduce all existence to a finite number of particles or waves, one can always ask, 'Why those particles?' or 'Why those waves?' " Physicist Stephen Hawking puts the puzzle a little differently, noting that even if he and his colleagues should one day succeed in their quest for a Grand Unified Theory—a single mathematical formula that would encompass all the laws of nature—we would still have no idea of why the universe goes to the bother of existing. Nor would a Theory of Everything bring us one step closer to unraveling the enigma of a thinking animal that longs to know the mind of God.

Alan Guth, a particle physicist at MIT, has probably come as close as anyone else to unscrewing the inscrutable. A refinement on the Big Bang, Guth's theory states that we live in an "inflationary universe" which bubbled out of something called a "false vacuum." At the moment, this is the *ne plus ultra* — the reigning interpretation of how it all began. Guth's equations show how, given the laws of nature as we know them, it really is possible for something to materialize from nothing. (This is because the universe only *appears* to be something; the positive energy of all the matter in the cosmos is precisely canceled by the gravitational force it exerts, whose energy is negative, so that in the peculiar accounting of physics, the sum total of everything that exists is zero.) "It is rather fantastic to realize that the laws of physics can describe how everything was created in a random quantum fluctuation out of nothing, and how over the course of 15 billion years, matter could organize in such complex ways that we have human beings sitting here," Guth enthuses. "Fantastic" may be an understatement. But then the question intrudes, who made the laws of nature? Guth confesses, "We are a long way from being able to answer that one!"

What do we really know about this strange and beautiful world in which we find ourselves? A poet says:

> *We glibly talk of nature's laws*
> *But do things have a natural cause?*
> *Black earth turned into yellow crocus*
> *Is undiluted hocus-pocus.*

The philosopher Bertrand Russell once remarked that the question of God had never particularly vexed him, but that there were certain ambiguities regarding the nature of mathematical axioms that threatened to unhinge his sanity. Like many young people, Russell was intolerant of ambiguity and set out on an expedition for absolute truth. Early in his career, he and Alfred North Whitehead wrote a treatise titled *Principia Mathematica*, which they hoped would establish a formal groundwork for all possible mathematical knowledge. It was only a few years after Russell and Whitehead had completed their monumental work that another thinker, Kurt Gödel (1906–1978), showed that even in the realm of pure mathematical logic, there is no such thing as ultimate truth. Everything rests on a turtle, who in turn rests on nothing.

In his book *Gödel, Escher, Bach: An Eternal Golden Braid*, Douglas R. Hofstadter explains that "a system of reasoning can be compared to an egg. An egg has a shell that protects its insides. If you want to ship the egg somewhere, though, you don't rely on the shell. You pack the egg in some sort of container, chosen according to how rough you expect the egg's voyage to be. To be extra careful, you may put the egg inside several nested boxes. However, no matter how many layers of boxes you pack your egg in, you can imagine some cataclysm which could break the egg . . . Similarly, one can never give an ultimate, absolute proof that a proof in some system is correct. Of course, one can give a proof of a proof, or a proof of a proof of a proof—but the validity of the outermost system always remains an unproven assumption, accepted on faith." At some point, Hofstadter says, you reach rock bottom, and there is no defense except shouting loudly, "I know I'm right!"

In the church I serve, we do occasionally shout loudly. While my flock tends to be fairly tolerant theologically, we can become quite dogmatic when choosing colors for the carpet. But we all know that shouting is no guarantee of being right. "I know I'm right," is what the Pope said to Galileo. Those are the famous last words. Many people imagine that they've found ultimate answers. In an 1894 speech, Albert Michaelson, the famous experimenter who measured the speed of light, stated that "the more important fundamental laws and facts of physical science have all been discovered, and these are now so firmly established that the possibility of their ever being supplanted in consequence of new discoveries is exceedingly remote." It was only a few years later that Einstein turned science on its head. In 1931 the physicist Arthur H. Compton stated positively that there existed three basic entities in the physical universe: protons, electrons and photons. The next year, James Chadwick at the Cavendish Laboratory discovered the neutron. Today scientists know more than ever about the fundamental building blocks of matter and energy that make up our universe, but they are as far as ever from arriving at ultimate answers. Few believe that any final truth is attainable. In the words of the chemist J.B.S. Haldane (1892–1964), "The universe is not only queerer than we suppose, but queerer than we can suppose."

There are a few people who seem to be immune to mystery and impervious to wonder. The critic Irving Babbit was of this temperament, for instance. He once remarked that he saw nothing remarkable about the facts of birth or death. How else would people come into the world, or leave it at the end?

Most people do wonder at life at least occasionally, however, and the most creative minds, whether in science or religion, seem to gaze out on the world with eyes that see the marvelous hidden behind the matter-of-fact. Bertrand Russell observed that original thinkers have "the faculty of not taking familiar things for granted. Newton wondered why apples fall; Einstein expressed 'surprised thankfulness' that four equal sides can make a square, since, in most of the universes he could imagine, there would be no such things as squares." In the words of the contemporary Jewish theologian Abraham Heschel, "The way to prayer leads through *acts of wonder* and *radical amazement*." Michael Polanyi, the philosopher of science, writes in a similar vein of Christian worship as being based upon "an eternal, never to be consummated hunch . . . It is like an obsession with a problem known to be insoluble, which yet follows, against reason, unswervingly, the heuristic command, 'Look at the unknown!' "

Science and religion have this in common: both are better at questioning our answers than at answering our questions. At their worst, each becomes a fixed body of knowledge, a rigid *corpus* of doctrine beyond criticism or contention. But ideally, each can lift us beyond the known, toward fresh visions of the real. Science does this through a process of falsification. Hypotheses can be invalidated but never conclusively verified. Thus the dream of discovering a Final Theory is likely to remain a dream—because every proposition in science contains at least a germ of tentativeness about it. Today's established consensus has a habit of becoming tomorrow's discard. And theology is not so different in this respect. "Proofs" of God's existence have seldom been convincing, and every statement about the ineffable by its very nature is partial, imperfect, incomplete. Like physicists, who know that an electron can sometimes be likened to a particle and at other times compared to a wave, but realize that neither simile matches the utter peculiarity of the subatomic world, theologians need to recognize that creeds and doctrines are far from capturing the reality they purport to describe. The *via negativa,* which simply asserts what God is *not,* may be the closest anyone can come to speaking definitively of the divine.

Faith comes to us in the form of questions and quandaries. In the book of Job, for example, God speaks in the interrogative mood rather than the imperative. Job is a man who feels mistreated; he is also a figure in search of answers. And in reply to Job's repeated requests for a divine audience, the Holy One eventually responds. But God's words are not punctuated with exclamation points. They are queries, not declarations. So God does not ever really satisfy Job's petition for a redress of grievances, nor offer any cut-and-dried explanation of how the world works. Rather, the voice from the whirlwind admonishes Job: "Brace yourself and stand up like a man; I will ask questions and you will answer." In the epiphany that follows—the longest and most grandiose to be found anywhere within the pages of scripture— Job is asked to consider his place within the awe-ful scale of the cosmos. "Where were you when I laid the earth's foundations?" God asks. "Who watched over the birth of the sea, when it burst in flood from the womb? Have you comprehended the vast expanse of the world?" A lengthy list of inquiries ensues. "Who sired the drops of dew? Do you know when the mountain goats are born, or attend the wild doe when she is in labor?" What do you really know about this incredible world you inhabit, God seems to ask Job. And as a result of this relentless quizzing, Job is finally reconciled—not because he has been given any answers or rationalizations that could account for his fate, but because he has been forced to encounter the mystery of things at deeper, more daunting levels.

Einstein was one who cultivated a taste for mystery. In the last decades of his life, he was regarded as a bit of a crank by most other physicists, bent upon a lonely, seemingly quixotic quest for a unified field theory when the vanguard of science was busy advancing in other directions. Now, fifty years later, physicists have rejoined Einstein's pursuit, understanding that while he never did obtain his elusive quarry, he was at least asking the right questions, drawn on by an almost romantic attraction. "The most beautiful thing we can experience is the mysterious," he wrote.

> *It is the source of all true art and science. He to whom this emotion is a stranger, who can no longer pause to wonder and stand rapt in awe, is as good as dead: his eyes are closed. This insight into the mystery of life, coupled though it be with fear, has also given rise to religion. To know that what is impenetrable to us*

really exists, manifesting itself as the highest wisdom
and the most radiant beauty which our dull faculties
can comprehend only in their most primitive forms —
this knowledge, this feeling, is at the center of true
religiousness.

Such religiousness, for Einstein at least, implied humility, along with scorn for those who pretended to have attained to insights beyond their powers. In 1951, the great physicist reflected that "Fifty years of conscious brooding have brought me no closer to the answer to the question what are light quanta? Of course, today every rascal thinks he knows the answer, but he is deluding himself."

Many a rascal even now claims to know the thoughts of God. Some wear clerical collars and preach with great authority. But if Einstein was still so far from understanding photons or the nature of light, how much farther are we from delving the final riddle of our existence? Those who think they can delimit and define the ultimate are deluding themselves — for God by definition is the reality that defies and surpasses human comprehension. That reality has been called by many names — Yahweh, Allah, Vishnu — but none of these are God's names. Rather, these are our names for the unnamable, conventional rubrics that point toward what is unconventional and inexhaustible, beyond categorization.

At the end of his life, Isaac Newton had this to say. "I do not know what I may appear to the world; but to myself I seem to have been only like a boy playing on the seashore, and diverting myself in now and then finding a smoother pebble or a prettier shell than ordinary, whilst the great ocean of truth lay all undiscovered before me." Most of Newton's other pronouncements sound dated to the modern ear. But this simple confession of modesty is timeless, as pertinent now as the day it was written.

To see the wonder in each bit of time and space is indeed the occupation of a scientist or a saint. To perceive the mystery that lies behind and beneath this world is to live in a state of astonishment and reverence for What Is. All things exist, yet only we, the human creation, are fully aware that we exist. To become completely conscious of the mystery within us and around us, to look steadily at the unknown, to contemplate the infinite heights and depths of existence is what it means to be most deeply human and most genuinely alive.

Someone once defined spirituality as the practice of "awe-robics." If we are aware and awake to wonder, then it becomes possible to cultivate what Einstein called "a holy curiosity" We can avoid the pitfalls of arrogance and self-certainty and instead accept the mystery in which we live and move with serenity and trust. Our response to the unknown is not anxiety, but appreciation mixed with the anticipation of discovery and enlightenment. Amazement and astonishment become everyday reactions to the world around us. We can cease looking for marvels in faraway places or esoteric sources, for marvels are all around. "Why, who makes much of a miracle?" the poet Walt Whitman asked.

> As to me, I know of nothing else but miracles,
> Whether I walk the streets of Manhattan,
> Or dart my sight over the roofs of houses toward the
>   sky,
> Or wade with naked feet along the beach, just in the
>   edge of the water,
> Or stand under trees in the woods . . .
> To me, every hour of the light and dark is a miracle,
> Every cubic inch of space is a miracle,
> Every square yard of the surface of the earth is spread
>   with the same,
> Every foot of the interior swarms with the same;
> Every spear of grass . . .
> What stranger miracles are there?

The words "marvel" and "miracle" come from an ancient Indo-European root that means to laugh or smile. From the same root comes our word "admiration." To wonder is to be glad at life. To admire, to hold worthy, to worship, is to taste the fresh goodness of the world in which we live.

The Buddha told this parable: a traveler, fleeing a tiger who was chasing him, ran till he came to the edge of a cliff. There he caught hold of a thick vine, and swung himself over the edge. Above him the tiger snarled. Below him he heard another snarl, and behold, there was another tiger, peering up at him. The vine suspended him midway between two tigers. Two mice, a white mouse and a black mouse, began to gnaw at the vine. He could see they were quickly eating it through. Then in front of him on the cliff side he saw a luscious bunch of grapes. Holding onto the vine with one hand, he reached and picked the grapes with the other. How delicious!

Life is sweet, and we realize it most clearly in those moments when we become aware that it is a mystery and a gift. We realize it most clearly in those moments when we're dangling over the abyss, when we become aware that simply to exist is a rare privilege, an astounding and continuous miracle, when we realize that it actually is "elephants all the way down"!

THE FUTURE OF FAITH

Sigmund Freud was merely echoing the received opinion of the day when he predicted in *The Future of an Illusion* that religion was becoming a relic of the past. In fact, he boldly compared his own theories to those of Copernicus and Darwin in propelling the human race beyond the magical thinking of childhood — the infantile supposition that we occupy the world's center-point — toward a sadder but wiser estimate of our own place in the cosmos. Belief in God — like belief in elves or leprechauns — was supposed to be the vanishing vestige of a primitive mentality. As recently as 1966, *TIME Magazine* could run a headline asking "Is God Dead?", prompting a parody from the religious journal *Motive:*

11

UNITED PRESS INTERNATIONAL—God, creator of the universe, principal deity of the world's Jews, ultimate reality of Christians and most eminent of all divinities, died late yesterday during major surgery undertaken to correct a massive diminishing influence.

But the rumors of God's demise turned out to be greatly exaggerated, and religion is flourishing as never before. Meanwhile, Freud's reputation and influence have undergone a major revision. Far from representing a scientific approach to unpacking human personality, psychoanalysis now seems more like an artifact of *fin de siècle* Vienna.

Freud was confident that his own "talking cure" would eventually be replaced by methods that could reduce psychology to nervous physiology. And some modern researchers claim to have discovered a "God circuit" within the brain that is the source of "unitive experiences" such as those attested in states of relaxed meditation by Tibetan monks. Andrew Newberg, a physician at the University of Pennsylvania, has used brain-imaging techniques to pinpoint an "orientation area" near the top and rear of the cerebrum that he believes is the source of the oceanic feeling. This region is responsible for weaving sensory input into an awareness of personal boundaries, and when it is disturbed, the line between oneself and the surrounding environment begins to blur. The result is a sensation of unity with all creation. Newberg calls his discipline "neuro-theology" and claims the nervous system is hard-wired for religious belief. But how does the monk's purposeful concentration interrupt neural circuits that are supposedly pre-programmed? The conclusion that spiritual awareness is nothing but the activity of brain waves and electrical impulses is like saying the works of Shakespeare are "nothing but" scribbles on paper. Language is associated with specific regions of the brain, too, but that does not come close to exhausting its meaning or significance.

Neuro-theology notwithstanding, belief in God will almost certainly be part of the human future, and the only question is what form that belief will take. Many will undoubtedly cling to the old formulas. A Sufi tale relates that Moses once admonished a humble shepherd whom he overheard offering to comb God's hair, wash God's robe and kiss God's hand, calling the man a blasphemer. But the Eternal One spoke to Moses and corrected him. "Thus hast thou driven away a worshiper from the nearest to Me that he could approach. There is a gradation in all men; each will perceive what he can perceive, and at the stage at which he can perceive it." If the scientific advances of the past century have done nothing to dampen the appeal of a naive, pre-critical faith, it is doubtful that any forthcoming discoveries will do so. For many, a God who "walks with me and talks with me" will continue to bring comfort.

Atheism will also remain with us. Disavowal of the gods has been a part of the scene at least since the collapse of the pantheon of ancient Greece. Yet card-carrying atheists today are relatively few in number. The American Humanist Association boasts a membership of just above five thousand, compared to over nineteen million for the Southern Baptist Convention. Those who demand logical demonstration or tangible proof of God's existence are secure in the redoubt of doubt, making atheism an unassailable intellectual position. And large numbers of people live morally upright, apparently satisfying lives WBOD ("without-benefit-of-deity"). But the hardy souls who can thrive in such a spiritual vacuum will probably always be in a minority. And in practice many atheists and agnostics can be as doctrinaire as the true believers they deride.

Between these two extremes there will be no real meeting of the minds. But in the muddled middle, where most people search for meaning, the faith of tomorrow is in ferment, as the rift that so long divided science and religion finally begins to mend. That fissure dates back to the nineteenth century, with the first rumblings from the modern study of geology. The layers of sedimentation and the timetables of erosion hinted at a story far older than any recorded in Holy Writ. Then Darwinism hit like an earthquake, and the aftershocks were immediate. Many lost their faith, while others who remained loyal to tradition grew fearful or suspicious of the entire scientific enterprise. In the twentieth century, by contrast, the advent of relativity and quantum theory scarcely registered on the religious Richter scale. For one thing, Einstein and Heisenberg proved harder to understand than Darwin, who knew very little math and required none of his readers. By that time, moreover, religious leaders and scientific thinkers had virtually stopped talking to each other. It took decades for the philosophical implications of the new physics to begin to penetrate the seminaries and divinity schools. But as science left behind the mechanistic, materialistic and reductionistic constructs that were so inimical to religious belief, a new synthesis seemed possible. Some even said that if physicists were ever finally successful in scaling the highest pinnacles of knowledge, they would discover a band of mystics already waiting at the top. Scientists and theologians, who almost closed the door to communication a hundred years earlier, were engaged in new and earnest conversation as the twentieth century passed its midpoint and bore down on the millennium.

Ralph Burhoe (1911–1997), founder of the Institute on Religion in an Age of Science, was among the pioneers in this dialogue. Forced to abandon his theological education by the Depression, Burhoe never did attain a formal degree of any kind. But as a meteorologist at Harvard's Blue Hill Observatory and later the first executive officer of the American Academy of Arts and Sciences, he came into contact with many outstanding scientists of the time, enlisting their support as editors and referees for *Zygon: The Journal of Religion and Science*, the first peer-reviewed periodical in the field. A recent issue contained an article on "Divine Action and Quantum Possibility" along with the intriguing title "Is the Biosphere Doing Theology?" Burhoe was among the early recipients of the Templeton Prize for Progress in Religion in recognition of his efforts.

Since then over twenty others have been similarly honored. Established by financier John Templeton, the annual award that bears his name deliberately exceeds the Nobel in cash value, carrying a premium of £700,000 sterling, and is intended to rival the better-known prize in prestige as well. Most Templeton honorees are multidisciplinary in approach. Arthur Peacocke, the 2001 winner, was senior lecturer in biophysical chemistry at the University of Birmingham in England before pursuing his Diploma in Theology. John Polkinghorne, who won the following year, had a distinguished career in physics at Cambridge before being ordained as an Anglican priest. Not since Isaac Newton's day, perhaps, has there been such a comfortable fit between the dual vocations of scientist and cleric.

That fit could also describe Robert Russell, an ordained minister in the United Church of Christ with a Ph.D. in physics who now directs the Center for Theology and the Natural Sciences, affiliated with the Graduate Theological Union in Berkeley. "As in bridge building," says Russell, "each community, the religious and the scientific, must find bedrock in its own world, yet each must venture out toward the other, hoping that one day the two will meet at the keystone." Russell's end of the bridge clearly has its foundation in faith.

But scientists are also hard at work from their side. In 1995, the American Academy for the Advancement of Science organized its Program of Dialogue on Science, Ethics and Religion. Seminars on "Primatology and Human Nature" explore the issue of what it means to be human. Conferences on "Cosmic Questions" probe the riddles, *Did the Universe Have a Beginning?*, *Was the Universe Designed?*, and *Are We Alone?* Beyond the ivory tower, the program initiated a series of public meetings with local clergy in Kansas to better understand their concerns about teaching evolution in the schools.

All are voices in a growing discussion—a conversation that began hesitantly but that has steadily gathered energy and momentum in the last twenty years. A quick search of the internet, for example, yields over a million sites that touch on "science and religion." Where this dialogue will lead is unclear. But the longstanding impasse between the two camps looks much less impassable than before. Perhaps, as the French priest and paleontologist Pierre Teilhard de Chardin (1881–1955) remarked, there is not finally that much difference between research and adoration. Across the narrowing divide, the chatter is starting to hum.

This book is one more contribution to the buzz. And my own interest in writing on this topic may be indicative of the experience of others, as well. As a child, I attended Sunday School regularly. I'm sure the teachers were warm and well-intentioned for the most part. But the Bible stories we learned seemed much less real or vibrant than what I was learning about fossils and stars and planets and other living creatures. The "vocational inventory" I took in high school said I should probably be a geologist when I grew up, and no one—least of all me—would have predicted that I would wind up as a clergyman. For even if I had wanted to believe in God as a youngster, I wasn't exposed to any models of divinity that seemed viable or congruent with what I was learning about the rest of the universe. I was curious about the ages of the rock, but couldn't care less about the Rock of Ages or the Old-Man-with-a-Beard. If you had asked me for a definition of faith, I probably would have agreed with Mark Twain's sardonic comment that "faith means believing what any darn fool knows ain't so."

Too many people are still stuck with that juvenile definition, I'm afraid. Millions have inklings and intuitions that there is "something more" to life, but are unable to accept the outworn theology of a pre-scientific past and remain unaware that anything new or better exists that might take its place. And so they turn to psychoanalysis or the other failed gods of recent decades, poor substitutes for an authentic spirituality.

Authentic religion has always had the role of orienting people in the cosmos. It has struggled to answer the primordial questions, Who are we? Where do we come from? Where do we fit in the larger scheme of things? And the answers that are arising today from cosmologists, physicists and biologists are not precisely the passwords that gave hope and serenity to former generations. But the good news is that science is once again beginning to affirm what religion at its best has always told us, that knowledge of the natural world need not be a source of disillusionment or disappointment. Indeed, the more we learn, the more reason we have to feel at home in the universe, related to all that is. And as we incorporate this knowledge more deeply into our hearts, we understand that in protecting the larger circle of life we are also preserving ourselves.

The meaning of existence is not multiple choice, but if it were, and if life were a test, there might be questions like the following on the final exam. Which of the following best describes our situation here?

a) *We are cells within the four-billion-year-old body of a living planet.*

b) *We are partners in an intricate but improvisational evolutionary dance.*

c) *We are Great Apes – complex yet lovable creatures who can therefore only be fully known through love.*

Are these scientific questions? Partly. Are they religious questions? Certainly. And the answer toward which many of the most original thinkers in both fields are now tending is *d) All of the above.* Far from being lost or adrift amid the immensities, human beings are expressions of the same creative energy that kindles the stars, worshipful beings in a firmament that rightfully evokes our feelings of kinship and communion, participants in an old but ongoing saga that we not only behold with bemused astonishment but in some mysterious manner help conceive and bring to birth.

In the conclusion to his book *Space, Time and Gravitation,* Sir Arthur Stanley Eddington (1882–1944), the astronomer whose measurements of the solar eclipse helped to confirm Einstein's General Theory of Relativity, wrote that this theorem "unified the great laws, which by the precision of their formulation and the exactness of their application have won the proud place in human knowledge which physical science holds today. And yet, in regard to the nature of things, this knowledge is only an empty shell—a form of symbols. It is knowledge of structural form, and not knowledge of content. All through the physical world runs that unknown content, which must surely be the stuff of our consciousness." He continued:

> *We have found a strange footprint on the shores of the unknown. We have devised profound theories, one after another, to account for its origin. At last, we have succeeded in reconstructing the creature that made the footprint. And Lo! it is our own.*

In the human mind, the universe is growing in awareness of itself. And as science progresses, that mind has begun to resolve a vision far more wondrous than the "wheels within wheels" of Ezekiel or the creaking machinery of an eighteenth-century clockwork. Far from being finished, the journey of faith may be just beginning. And if we have courage to follow it, the truth will set us free.

ISSUES FOR DISCUSSION

Readers are encouraged to use this book as a basis for group discussion, in interfaith study circles or within their own congregations. The questions below are intended to help get you underway.

Some of the questions included here are relatively cerebral. Others delve into the realm of personal feelings and demand a level of trust and self-disclosure among the participants. Those who have perused the preceding pages will undoubtedly bring issues of their own.

Two or three discussion items have been included for each of the various chapters, but group leaders are invited to use the prepared questions as a starting point only and are advised not to attempt to cover the entire list. The relationship between science and religion is an enormous topic, far larger than the scope of this book, and any one of these "points to ponder" could lead into a productive evening's conversation.

Pope John XXIII once said that "it takes many to be wise," and I firmly believe that our own faith can be enriched through the encounter with differing viewpoints. Remember to speak and listen respectfully. Your own intellectual and spiritual journey can undoubtedly be enhanced through the cross-pollination of ideas.

* * *

"Space is the Whom our loves are needed by," wrote the poet W.H. Auden. "Time is our choice of How to love and Why." Is scientific description of our world necessarily more precise than poetry? Or can poetic language point to aspects of reality that science misses?

Which is more dangerous: science or religion? Can you think of instances where the split between the two—blind faith or lame reasoning—has led to unhappy results?

A survey asked people to respond to the question: "Do you believe in God?" The next item on the questionnaire was, "Have you ever felt close to God?" Many people said they had felt close to God, without necessarily believing in the existence of a deity. Why might a person be able to experience God without being able to explain God? How would you answer the two survey questions?

How many of our current social ills—from drug addiction to depression to obsessive consumerism—stem from the lack of a satisfying spirituality? What are the benefits of developing a personal spiritual practice or participating in an organized religious community?

Psychologist Martin Seligman suggests that depression can be caused by the differing "explanatory styles" people employ to interpret their universe. A person who believes he is powerless or unimportant is more prone to despair than one who sees herself as powerful and contributing to the world's well-being. In what ways do the differing "explanatory styles" of science and religion make us feel either powerful or powerless, important or insignificant *vis-à-vis* the rest of the world?

Friedrich Schleiermacher defined religion as "the feeling of absolute dependence." Have you ever shared this feeling? How would you define religion?

What accounts for the rapid growth of fundamentalism in the last century? How is it that America, one of the world's most technologically sophisticated societies, is also home to a resurgence of religious reaction? What unmet human needs might be addressed by a literalistic or authoritarian belief system?

Physicist Stephen Weinberg criticizes religious liberals for being fuzzy-minded. "Many religious liberals today seem to think that different people can believe in differently mutually exclusive things without any of them being wrong. This one believes in reincarnation, that one in heaven and hell; a third believes in the extinction of the soul at death, but no one can be said to be wrong as long as everyone gets a satisfying spiritual rush." Is this a valid critique? Or is the mark of a mature faith the ability to hold several contradictory ideas in mind at the same time?

Erwin Schrödinger describes a "peak experience" of feeling connected to a larger, more lasting Self. What have been the peak experiences within your own spiritual journey? When and where have you felt related to a larger, more enduring reality?

Some people feel that space exploration is an adventure essential to the human spirit. Others regard it a waste of money better spent here on earth. What is your opinion?

How is religious belief related to, the same as or different from belief in the supernatural?

Do we inhabit a friendly universe or one hostile or indifferent to our humanity? Do you agree with Freeman Dyson that the cosmos in some inexplicable way "saw us coming"?

Lee Smolin suggests that science education turns off many students because the picture of the universe presented in the physics classroom has so little room for human values. What turned you on or turned you off in your educational encounters with science? How can we interest children in learning about the amazing universe we inhabit?

"Skepticism is a good instinct in both science and theology." But skepticism alone cannot lead to any positive affirmation about the world. How do you balance skepticism and the will to believe? Must all our beliefs be scientifically testable?

Corita Kent once remarked that "to believe in God is to have the great faith that somewhere, something is not stupid." How do you account for order, pattern and meaning in the cosmos? Who created beauty? The mathematical elegance that inheres in the structure of time and space? Or are these simply lucky accidents?

Biologist Richard Dawkins asserts that "The universe that we observe has precisely the properties we should expect if there is, at bottom, no design, no purpose, no evil, and no good, nothing but blind, pitiless indifference." How might a person of faith explain the presence of seemingly random tragedies in our lives?

Can atheists and agnostics (like Stephen Jay Gould) be considered to be "religious" in some sense? What is the difference between a "religious humanist" and a "secular humanist?"

C. S. Lewis writes that "in Christianity God is not a static thing—not even a person—but a dynamic, pulsating activity, a life, almost a kind of drama. Almost, if you will not think me irreverent, a kind of dance." Is the dance a helpful metaphor in imagining God? What other metaphors do you use to describe the nature of ultimate reality?

Competition is only one of the engines that drives evolutionary change. Cooperation is the other. To what extent is competition a "natural" instinct for humankind?

When does competition become counterproductive and unnatural?

Some feminists posit a "golden age" before the dawn of patriarchy when people lived in harmony with the earth. This was the era of goddess worship. Do you believe such a golden age ever really existed? Is a revival of goddess worship possible or desirable in modern times? Should God be conceived non-sexually or in androgynous terms?

How would our attitudes and behavior toward the natural world change if we came to believe that "life is a community, not a commodity?" In what ways does the economic marketplace make good decisions about the allocation of resources? In what ways is the market limited in its foresight and wisdom?

Some would say that nature is the primordial sacrament. Have you had spiritual or "transformative" experiences in relation to the natural world? Where in nature do you go to restore and freshen your own wellsprings?

Can other species be owned? Should genes be patented? And will how we answer these questions depend partly on how we conceive of Gaia?

One study shows that women may be better than men at remembering the emotional content of specific situations. Do you believe men and women experience and analyze the world in fundamentally different ways? Are there typically feminine and masculine forms of spirituality?

What constraints—if any—should be placed on the use of primates and other animals in experimental research? Do animals have "rights" or deserve legal protection against some forms of abuse?

Neurologist Oliver Sacks describes the case of a judge with a brain impairment that stripped him of the ability to feel emotion. "It might be thought that the absence of emotion, and of the biases that go with it, would have rendered him more impartial—indeed, uniquely qualified—as a judge. But he himself, with great insight, resigned from the bench, saying that he could no longer enter sympathetically into the motives of anyone concerned, and that since justice involved feeling, and not merely thinking, he felt that his injury totally disqualified him." Why would a judge's fact-finding ability suffer from an inability to feel emotion? Would a scientist's investigative powers be similarly impaired? When do emotions help us to see the world more clearly and when do they get in the way?

Can science ever be totally "objective" or "value free"? Or are hidden value judgments implied in every human enterprise? Do scientists carry a professional responsibility for the use or misuse of their research? Is the search for knowledge a good in and of itself, irrespective of how that knowledge is employed?

Process theology holds that the philosophy of materialism is mistaken. The basic constituents of reality are not enduring substances but evanescent events. What difference does it make whether we think the world is made of nouns or verbs? In what ways is the process perspective similar to Taoism, Buddhism and other schools of Eastern thought?

Process thought holds that, at some incipient level, everything is alive. The world is more like a great organism than like a great machine. Is this an accurate description of our universe? What are the strengths and limitations of the mechanistic model of reality?

Einstein once said, "Imagination is more important than knowledge. Knowledge is limited. Imagination encircles the world." Comment and discuss.

Do you believe in miracles? How do you define the miraculous?

Our answers may divide us, but our questions bring us together. Does the idea that God appears in the form of questions make sense to you? What questions in your own life have spurred you toward growth and change? What questions do you struggle with at this stage in your life?

What did you find most troublesome or challenging about *Science and the Search for God?* What other issues arose as you read this book?

BIBLIOGRAPHY

Arcadi, Adam, Daniel Robert and Christophe Boesch. "Buttress
    Drumming by Wild Chimpanzees: Temporal Patterning, Phrase
    Integration into Loud Calls, and Preliminary Evidence for
    Individual Distinctiveness," **Primates**, 39(4), 1998.

Armstrong, Karen. *A History of God,* Ballantine Books, New York,
    NY 1993.

Auden, W.H. *The Collected Poetry of W.H. Auden,* Random House,
    New York, NY 1945.

Barbour, Ian G. *Issues in Science and Religion,* Harper & Row, New
    York, NY 1966.

_____. *When Science Meets Religion,* HarperSanFrancisco, San
    Francisco, CA 2000.

Barlow, Maude, and Tony Clarke. *Blue Gold: The Battle Against Theft
    of the World's Water,* Stoddart Publishing, Toronto, Canada 2002

Barrow, John D. and Frank J. Tipler. *The Anthropic Cosmological
    Principle,* Oxford University Press, New York, NY 1986.

Berry, Thomas. *The Dream of the Earth,* Sierra Club Books, San
    Francisco, CA 1988.

Booth, Mark (ed.). *What I Believe: Thirteen Eminent People of Our Time
    Argue for Their Philosophy of Life,* Crossroad Publishing
    Company, New York, NY 1984.

Chardin, Teilhard de. *The Phenomenon of Man,* Harper Colophon
    Books, New York, NY 1965.

Clark, John Ruskin. *The Great Living System: The Religion Emerging
    from the Sciences,* Skinner House Books, Boston, MA 1977.

Clark, Ronald W. *The Survival of Charles Darwin: A Biography of a Man and an Idea,* Random House, New York, NY 1984.

Cobb, John B., Jr. "Hartshorne's Importance for Theology," in *The Library of Living Philosophers, v. XX,* Lewis Edwin Hahn (ed.), Open Court, La Salle, Illinois 1991.

Crick, Francis. *The Astonishing Hypothesis: The Scientific Search for the Soul,* Scribner, New York, NY 1993.

Christianson, Gale E. *In the Presence of the Creator: Isaac Newton and His Times,* The Free Press, New York, NY 1984.

Daly, Mary. *Beyond God the Father,* Beacon Press, Boston, MA 1973.

Darwin, Charles. *The Origin of Species,* Collier, New York, NY 1961.

Darwin, Francis (ed.). *Autobiography and Selected Letters of Charles Darwin,* Dover Publications, New York, NY 1958.

Dawkins, Richard. *The Blind Watchmaker,* Norton, New York, NY 1986.

Dennett, Daniel C. *Consciousness Explained,* Little, Brown, Boston, MA 1991.

Dillard, Annie. *Teaching A Stone To Talk: Expeditions and Encounters,* Harper & Row, New York, NY 1982.

Eddington, Sir Arthur Stanley. *Space, Time, and Gravitation: An Outline of General Relativity Theory,* Cambridge University Press, Cambridge, England 1953.

Eisler, Riane. *The Chalice and the Blade,* Harper & Row, San Francisco, CA 1987.

Eller, Cynthia. *The Myth of Matriarchal Prehistory,* Beacon Press, Boston, MA 2000.

Dyson, Freeman. *Disturbing the Universe,* Basic Books, Inc., New York, NY 1979.

Ferris, Timothy. *Coming of Age in the Milky Way,* William Morrow and Company, New York, NY 1988.

Fleck, Peter G. *The Mask of Religion,* Prometheus Books, Buffalo, NY 1980.

Folger, Tim, "Does the Universe Exist If We're Not Looking?" **Discover**, v. 23, n. 6, June 2002

Fouts, Roger, with Stephen Tukel Mills. *Next of Kin: What Chimpanzees Have Taught Me About Who We Are,* William Morrow and Company, New York, NY 1997.

Freud, Sigmund. *The Future of an Illusion,* Norton, New York, NY 1975.

Galdikas, Biruté. *Reflections of Eden: My Years with the Orangutans of Borneo,* Little, Brown, Boston, MA 1995.

Gardner, Martin (ed.). *The Sacred Beetle and other Great Essays in Science,* New American Library, New York, NY 1984.

_____. *The Whys of a Philosophical Scrivener,* Quill, New York, NY 1983.

Gleick, James. *Chaos: Making A New Science,* Viking, New York, NY 1987.

Goldenberg, Naomi. *Changing of the Gods,* Beacon Press, Boston, MA 1979.

Goodall, Jane. *The Chimpanzees of Gombe: Patterns of Behavior,* Belknap Press of Harvard University Press, Cambridge, MA 1986.

_____. *My Friends, The Wild Chimpanzees,* National Geographic Society, Washington, D.C. 1967

_____. *Reason for Hope: A Spiritual Journey,* Warner Books, New York, NY 1999.

Gould, Stephen Jay, "Human Equality is a Contingent Fact of History," **Natural History**, 93(11), November 1984.

_____. *I Have Landed: The End of a Beginning in Natural History,* Harmony Books, New York, NY 2002.

Greene, Brian. *The Elegant Universe: Superstrings, Hidden Dimensions, and the Quest for the Ultimate Theory,* Vintage Books, New York, NY 2000.

Gribbin, John. *Cosmic Coincidences: Dark Matter, Mankind and Anthropic Cosmology,* Bantam Books, New York, NY 1989.

_____. *In Search of Schrödinger's Cat: Quantum Physics and Reality,* Bantam Books, New York, NY 1984.

Griffin, David Ray. *Religion and Scientific Naturalism: Overcoming the Conflicts,* State University of New York Press, Albany, NY 2000.

Harrison, Edward. *Masks of the Universe,* MacMillan Publishing Company, New York, NY 1985.

Hartshorne, Charles. *Born To Sing: An Interpretation and World Survey of Bird Song,* Indiana University Press, Blooomington, IN 1973.

_____. *The Darkness and the Light,* State University of New York Press, Albany, NY 1990.

_____. *The Divine Relativity: A Social Conception of God,* Yale University Press, New Haven, CT 1948.

Hawking, Stephen. *A Brief History of Time: From the Big Bang to Black Holes,* Bantam Books, New York, NY 1988.

Henderson, Lawrence Joseph. *The Fitness of the Environment: An Inquiry into the Biological Significance of the Properties of Matter*

(With an Introduction by George Wald), Beacon Press, Boston, MA 1958.

Heschel, Abraham. *Quest for God: Studies in Prayer and Symbolism,* Crossroad, New York, NY 1990.

Hofstadter, Douglas R. *Gödel, Escher, Bach: An Eternal Golden Braid,* Basic Books, New York, NY 1979.

Hughes, Robert. *The Shock of the New,* McGraw-Hill, New York, NY 1976.

James, William. *The Varieties of Religious Experience,* MacMillan Publishing Company, New York, NY 1961.

Jammer, Max. *Einstein and Religion: Physics and Theology,* Princeton University Press, Princeton, NJ 1999.

Jeans, Sir James. *The Mysterious Universe,* MacMillan Publishing Company, New York, NY 1932.

Kelly, Frank, Stephen Jay Gould, James Anthony Ryan, and Debora Rindge. *Frederic Edwin Church,* Smithsonian Institution Press, Washington, D.C. 1989.

Kunzig, Robert. "The Glue That Holds the World Together," **Discover**, v. 21, n. 7, July 2000.

Lemley, Brad, "Guth's Grand Guess," **Discover**, v. 23, n. 4, April 2002

Lingelbach, Jenepher. *Hands-On Nature: Information and Activities for Explaining the Environment with Children,* Vermont Institute of Natural Science, Woodstock, VT 1986.

Lovelock, James E. *Gaia: A New Look at Life on Earth,* Oxford University Press, Oxford, England 1979

Montgomery, Sy. *Walking with the Great Apes: Jane Goodall, Dian Fossey, Biruté Galdikas,* Houghton Mifflin, Boston, MA 1991.

Mercader, Julio, Melissa Panger, Christophe Boesche, "Excavation of a Chimpanzee Stone Tool Site in the African Rainforest," **Science**, 296(5572), May 24, 2002.

Mowat, Farley. *Woman in the Mists: The Story of Dian Fossy and the Mountain Gorillas of Africa,* Warner Books, New York, NY 1987.

Newberg, Andrew. *Why God Won't Go Away: Brain Science and the Biology of Belief,* Ballantine Books, New York, NY 2001.

Parnell, Peter, "How Does A Photon Decide Where To Go? That's the Quantum Mystery," **New York Times,** April 21, 2002.

Polkinghorne, John. *Belief in God in an Age of Science,* Yale University Press, New Haven, CT 1998.

Price, Lucien. *Dialogues of Alfred North Whitehead,* Little, Brown, Boston, MA 1954.

Russell, Bertrand. *A History of Western Philosophy,* Simon and Schuster, New York, NY 1945.

Schrödinger, Erwin. *What Is Life?* Doubleday, Garden City, NJ 1956.

Singer, Peter. *Animal Liberation,* Avon Books, New York, NY 1975.

Smolin, Lee. *The Life of the Cosmos,* Oxford University Press, New York, NY 1997.

Spretnak, Charlene. *Lost Goddesses of Early Greece,* Beacon Press, Boston, MA 1992.

Stone, Merlin. *When God Was A Woman,* Dial Press, New York, NY 1976.

Swimme, Brian. *The Universe is a Green Dragon: A Cosmic Creation Story,* Bear & Co., Santa Fe, NM 1985.

Thomas, Lewis. *Lives of a Cell: Notes of a Biology Watcher,* Viking Press, New York, NY 1974.

Tillich, Paul. *Theology of Culture,* Oxford University Press, London, England 1959.

Tully, Shawn, "Water, Water Everywhere," **Fortune**, v. 141, issue 10, May 15, 2000.

Wise, Stephen. *Rattling the Cage,* Perseus Publishing, Cambridge, MA 2000.

Weinberg, Stephen. *Dreams of a Final Theory,* Pantheon Books, New York, NY 1992.

Wheeler, John Archibald. *At Home in the Universe,* American Institute of Physics, Woodbury, NY 1996.

Whitman, Walt. *Leaves of Grass,* Modern Library, New York, NY 1950.

Whitehead, Alfred North. *Process and Reality,* Harper and Brothers, New York, NY 1957.

Wilson, Edward O. *The Future of Life,* Alfred A. Knopf, New York, NY 2002.

OTHER BOOKS BY GARY KOWALSKI

The Souls of Animals

Goodbye Friend:
Healing Wisdom for Anyone Who Has Ever Lost a Pet

Green Mountain Spring and Other Leaps of Faith

The Bible According to Noah:
Theology as if Animals Mattered

ALSO BY LANTERN BOOKS

Keith Akers
The Lost Religion of Jesus
Simple Living and Nonviolence in Early Christianity

Akers argues that Jewish Christianity was vegetarian and practiced pacifism and communal living. "A whole new conception of Christianity." —**Walter Wink**

Judy Carman
Peace To All Beings
Veggie Soup for the Chicken's Soul
Foreword by Gene Bauston

This visionary guidebook shows how animal rights and liberation are an essential part of any movement that is working to make the world a better place. It is a valuable aid for anyone seeking to live in harmony with the values of compassion, nonviolence and reverence for all life.

J. R. Hyland
God's Covenant with Animals
A Biblical Basis for the Humane Treatment of All Creatures

The Bible, argues Hyland, calls upon human beings to stop their violence and abuse of each other and other creatures. "A daring and profoundly original work . . ." — **Stephen H. Webb**, author, *On God and Dogs*

Glen Peter Kezwer
Meditation, Oneness and Physics
A Journey through the Laboratories of Physics and Meditation

An entertaining, informative and thought-provoking insight into the connections between the sciences of physics and meditation based on the author's own direct experience.

Martin Rowe, Editor
The Way of Compassion
Vegetarianism, Environmentalism, Animal Advocacy, and Social Justice
A Stealth Technologies Book

"Sophisticated but not inaccessible, this . . . important and deeply engaging book belongs in all but the smallest libraries." — *Library Journal*